# ON PURPOSE WOMAN

## THE COMPLETE HOLISTIC GUIDE FOR SPIRITUAL ENTREPRENEURS

### GINNY ROBERTSON

FEATURING: LATISHA BOYD-POTTS, LAURA DI FRANCO, GAIL DIXON, MELISSA HARRIS, DR. CARLA JOHNSTON, OLIVIA A. JONES, GURPREET JUNEJA, DR. SREE MELETH, LAURIE MORIN, PAT PERRIER, REV. MARY PERRY, DR. MARIA PETRUCCI, LILIA SHOSHANNA RAE, TAMARA ROBINSON, JACQUELINE R. SCOTT, JEAN WRIGHT, KATHRYN YARBOROUGH

# ON PURPOSE WOMAN

## THE COMPLETE HOLISTIC GUIDE FOR SPIRITUAL ENTREPRENEURS

### GINNY ROBERTSON

FEATURING: LATISHA BOYD-POTTS, LAURA DI FRANCO, GAIL DIXON, MELISSA HARRIS, DR. CARLA JOHNSTON, OLIVIA A. JONES, GURPREET JUNEJA, DR. SREE MELETH, LAURIE MORIN, PAT PERRIER, REV. MARY PERRY, DR. MARIA PETRUCCI, LILIA SHOSHANNA RAE, TAMARA ROBINSON, JACQUELINE R. SCOTT, JEAN WRIGHT, KATHRYN YARBOROUGH

On Purpose Woman

The Complete Holistic Guide for Spiritual Entrepreneurs

Ginny Robertson

©Copyright 2023 Ginny Robertson

Published by Brave Healer Productions

All rights reserved. No part of this book may be used or reproduced by any means, graphic, electronic, or mechanical, including photocopying, recording, taping, or by any information storage retrieval system without the written permission of the publisher, except in the case of brief quotations embodied in critical articles and reviews.

Paperback ISBN: 978-1-961493-10-0

eBook ISBN: 978-1-961493-09-4

# DISCLAIMER

This book offers words of wisdom with regard to physical, mental, emotional, and spiritual wellbeing and is designed for educational purposes only. You should not rely on this information as a substitute for, nor does it replace professional medical or business advice, diagnosis, or treatment. If you have concerns or questions about your health, business, or mental wellbeing, you should always consult with a physician, other healthcare professional, or business professional. Do not disregard, avoid or delay obtaining medical or business-related advice from your healthcare or business professional because of something you may have read here. The use of any information provided in this book is solely at your own risk.

Developments in research may impact the health, business, and life advice that appears here. No assurances can be given that the information contained in this book will always include the most relevant findings or developments with respect to the particular material.

Having said all that, know that the authors here have shared their tools, practices, and knowledge with you with a sincere and generous intent to assist you on your journey to being unstoppable in business and life. Please contact them with any questions you may have about the techniques or information they have provided. They will be happy to assist you further!

# DEDICATION

For Don.

You're my lover, my rock, my muse, my greatest fan, and my spiritual partner on this beautiful and sometimes messy journey called life.

I could fill these pages with all the reasons I dedicate this book to you, but you already know.

So, I'll just leave this here:

*And then my soul saw you and it kind of went, Oh, there you are. I've been looking for you.*

~ Iain Thomas

# TABLE OF CONTENTS

### INTRODUCTION | i

---

Chapter 1

### NETWORKING WITH HEART | 1

CREATING CONNECTIONS THAT MATTER

By Ginny Robertson

---

Chapter 2

### CLARIFY WHAT YOU WANT | 11

HOW TO ATTRACT CLIENTS AND GROW YOUR DIVINELY INSPIRED BUSINESS

By Kathryn Yarborough

---

Chapter 3

### THE WRITE CONNECTION WITH SPIRIT | 20

HOW TO CHANNEL AND SHARE WORDS THAT GROW YOUR BUSINESS

By Laura Di Franco, MPT, Publisher

---

Chapter 4

### THE CRISPY YOGI | 32

BATTLING BURNOUT, GRIEF, AND INJURY

By Pat Perrier, MA, MBA, E-RYT 500

Chapter 5

## PUT YOURSELF FIRST | 40

UNLOCKING PASSION, PLEASURE, AND DESIRES
BY FOCUSING ON YOURSELF

By Tamara Robinson, Sex & Intimacy Coach

---

Chapter 6

## ESCAPE THE FEAR AND DO IT AFRAID | 49

DEVELOP DISCERNMENT, FIND YOUR PURPOSE,
AND CHANGE STRESS INTO JOY

By LaTisha Boyd-Potts, MSW, AMHFA, YMHFA

---

Chapter 7

## JOURNEY TO WHOLENESS | 57

THE PATH TO SELF-ACCEPTANCE AND
CREATING THE BUSINESS YOU LOVE

By Jacqueline (Jackie) R. Scott, JD, ML

---

Chapter 8

## CLARIFY WHAT YOU WANT | 66

THE FIRST STEP TO FINDING YOUR PURPOSE
AND REACHING YOUR GOALS

By Maria Petrucci, D.C.

Chapter 9
## **CHANGE TALK | 75**
5 KEYS TO MASTERING CHANGE
By Gail Dixon

Chapter 10
## **TRUSTING SPIRIT | 83**
AMPLIFY BUSINESS GROWTH THROUGH ANGEL CONNECTIONS
By Rev. Mary Perry, Angel Intuitive and Healer

Chapter 11
## **YOUR ORIGIN STORY | 92**
HOW TO BRING YOUR WHOLE AUTHENTIC SELF TO YOUR BUSINESS
By Laurie Morin

Chapter 12
## **ALLOWING THE AUTHENTIC YOU! | 100**
THE SECRET TO ATTRACTING MORE CLIENTS
By Dr. Sree Meleth

Chapter 13
## **THE CONFIDENCE CONUNDRUM | 108**
HOW TO CHANGE YOUR MINDSET TO GET WHAT YOU WANT
By Jean Wright

Chapter 14

**CULTIVATING AN AGING SPIRIT | 116**

THE HIDDEN POSSIBILITIES OF CHRONIC ILLNESS

By Carla Johnston, DCN, MA, MS, CNS, LDN

---

Chapter 15

**DREAMING THE IMPOSSIBLE DREAM | 126**

HOW PRAYER WILL TRANSFORM YOUR MIND AND
HELP YOU THRIVE IN LIFE'S TRANSITIONS

By Olivia A. Jones, Independent Beauty Consultant, MPA

---

Chapter 16

**TIME TO SHOW UP | 135**

IF NOT NOW, THEN WHEN?

By Gurpreet Juneja

---

Chapter 17

**FILL YOUR WELL | 145**

USING ART, BEAUTY, AND NATURE
FOR INSPIRATION AND PEACE OF MIND

By Melissa Harris

Chapter 18
## SEE YOURSELF AS ANGELS SEE YOU | 154
### SUCCEED IN YOUR SOUL'S PURPOSE
By Lilia Shoshanna Rae

## TAKE AN IMPORTANT NEXT STEP | 162
### SURROUND YOURSELF WITH OTHER ON PURPOSE WOMEN
By Ginny Robertson

## IN GRATITUDE | 167

## ABOUT THE AUTHOR | 169

# INTRODUCTION

My vision for this book is to bring brilliant women entrepreneurs together to share their wisdom and provide guidance to those desiring to live on purpose and grow or create a heart-centered business. Thank you to everyone who said yes!

It was easier for me to write this book's first and last chapters than it is to write this introduction. The voices in my head are having a battle.

*I should start by defining spiritual entrepreneur, but to do that, I should first define spiritual. But how can I define either of those when both are subjective? I'm not going to tell anyone what to believe. I don't want anyone to think this is about religion. But wait! Each author's personal relationship with her faith may come out in their chapter, and that's okay. What about purpose? Should I define an on-purpose woman? But wait, that's subjective too.*

*What's my job here anyway?*

This goes on for a while. This is only a tiny piece of the inner dialogue that's getting in the way of clarity about why I chose to be this book's lead author and why this title. It's a necessary process. The critical inner dialogue must play out so I can hear my inner wisdom.

*What's my job here anyway?*

With a clear head, I know that my job in writing this introduction *is* to define the words spiritual entrepreneur and on-purpose woman from my perspective. Since I can only write from my point of view and life experiences, it's all I've got.

For me, it's simple. I'm an on-purpose woman because I'm doing what I feel is mine to do. The quest to find purpose has become complicated, but it doesn't have to be. I find purpose in my daily life: the joyful, the painful, the exciting, and the mundane.

While it may be a spiritual mountaintop experience for some—where a voice comes down from the sky and tells you exactly why you're here—for most of us, it's about getting in touch with what makes our heart sing, gives us a deep sense of fulfillment, and points to ways we can make a difference. It still felt like a spiritual experience, but I didn't wait for the booming voice to give me my divine assignment. I listened to that still, small voice within for the clues because I already knew the answers. And you know your answers too.

Purpose is fluid, and the forms can change. My purpose is to give women opportunities to be seen and heard so they can make their unique impact. This has driven my work with the On Purpose Woman Global Community for 23 years. During my career in corporate finance, I mentored women and helped them grow personally and advance in their careers. In my position as a facilitator of personal growth seminars, I supported women in reaching beyond perceived limits and acknowledging and owning their power. And I have been a champion of women and girls for as long as I can remember. Same purpose but different forms.

Spirituality, for me, is knowing that I'm part of something greater. We become spiritual entrepreneurs by living our purpose and serving through our businesses.

The authors in this book are here to support your journey as a spiritual entrepreneur. Our shared experiences may help you avoid pitfalls, learn practical skills, understand why you chose your work, and move forward with grace, ease, and joy. As you go through these pages, keep an open mind about what's possible and be willing to dream big!

The world needs you and your gifts. Let's do this!

*There are two ways of spreading light: to be the candle or the mirror that reflects it.*

~ Edith Wharton

CHAPTER 1

# NETWORKING WITH HEART

## CREATING CONNECTIONS THAT MATTER

Ginny Robertson

## MY STORY

*Beam me up, Scotty. There's no intelligent life down here.* These are my thoughts as I wander from room to room, searching for a familiar, friendly face.

While I later learned that phrase was never spoken in an episode of Star Trek, it was commonly attributed to Captain Kirk and perfectly describes my feelings. I'm not questioning the intelligence of those around me, but as I roam the rooms, I want to be anywhere but here. I'm sure everyone knows everyone except me. I spot my cousin, Linda. I rarely see her and don't know her well, but she's my best friend right now.

"Whew," I say. "I'm happy to see someone I know." We update each other on our families and what we've been up to. It becomes apparent that she's way more comfortable in this environment than I am. Not wanting to monopolize her time, I quietly left the networking event I convinced myself I should attend.

*What a waste of time and money,* I tell myself on the drive home. I'm disappointed that I don't have anything to show for it.

This happened the same year I created what is now called the On Purpose Woman Global Community. While I loved the networking gatherings I hosted and the connections I made, I often got overwhelmed when attending other business networking events.

*I'll be more selective in the future and pick my events wisely, and I need a strategy.* So, I sign up for an event that's happening the following week. I typically avoid happy hour networking. I'm not a fan of the combination of alcohol and small talk. However, I feel pulled to attend. I think about how I might do it differently this time (remember, I need a strategy). I call a friend who's also an entrepreneur. "I need to get out there and meet some new women. Will you go with me?" I ask. "Of course," she replies. "I love events like this." I invite two more friends, and we all agree to meet in the parking lot. "I have a plan," I tell them.

"What's your plan, Ginny, and why do you think you need one?" asks my friend Karen as soon as she sees me. Karen is wildly comfortable meeting strangers, the kind of woman who talks to the wall and the wall replies. She doesn't need a plan. She shows up comfortable with who she is and always seems to have a great time. "Let's just go in and have fun," I say. "That's my plan." But that's not the whole plan. I'm keeping that to myself for now.

We arrive a bit early. I introduce myself to a woman who's alone. I feel a connection, chat with her, and introduce her to one of my friends. Then I leave them and look for someone else to talk with. I introduce that woman to another friend. Before long, my friends and the other two women bring other women to meet me. This goes on for a couple of hours. I'm having a great time, and my vibe attracts the coolest women!

I leave that event with a few quality business cards, and my new connections are excited about attending one of my gatherings.

These two networking experiences happened just a week apart and couldn't have been more different. I was miserable before, during, and after the first event and excited before, during, and after the second one.

## MY EXPERIENCE

I dreaded attending the first event because I didn't know what to expect or who would be there. Since I wasn't excited, I arrived late. It was tough walking in and feeling like everyone knew everyone. It was also a button-down event, and I felt out of place. After leaving my corporate gig nine years earlier, I had given away my business suits and vowed never to buy or wear one again. I'd glommed onto my cousin and made no effort to meet anyone else.

I was excited about attending the second event because my friends would be there. While I didn't plan to hang with just them all night, they were a safety net. As soon as I walked in, I saw a woman standing alone. I knew how that felt, so I introduced myself. She was grateful because she didn't know anyone else there. This started a chain of events that turned into a fun and productive evening because I'd created an intention for how I wanted to participate.

But something else was being uncovered.

My authentic Self hadn't shown up at that first event. I realized that in my zeal to get out there and meet more women because I thought it was the only way to grow my business, I'd lost sight of the reason I started the On Purpose Woman Global Community in the first place. My mission to give women a safe space to show up, practice being who they are, and make deep, authentic connections was woven through all I did within my community. But I wasn't living it outside of that safe space. I thought I should talk to every woman at this event and tell them what I do. This came from listening to yet another male business guru who preached, "Networking is a numbers game. You talk to enough people, you're bound to get a few to say yes." This notion and the sea of suits I found myself in were not aligned with my soul's purpose. I couldn't do it. So, I sabotaged the evening.

I was relaxed at the second event. It was light and informal. I was giving and sharing and helping others feel comfortable and have fun. I was listening more than talking. My only agenda was to be fully present and enjoy myself. My vibe attracted the right and perfect women. And the best part is that I did it with ease and grace. This is networking with heart.

Networking with heart is focusing on what you have to offer the person across from you, not what you can get from them. It's having the courage to show up authentically and being genuinely interested in others. It feels incredible when two or more of us operate from that same heart space.

## THE DESIRE FOR DEEP CONNECTION

We women desire deep, authentic personal connections with other women. Our work is a significant part of our identity as spiritual entrepreneurs. Our business connections must be as broad, deep, and genuine as our personal connections. We long to feel valued and supported, to share our thoughts, emotions, and lives, and feel needed. These desires reflect a fundamental human need to be with others and create a sense of belonging. The results can be magical when we seek these connections consciously, with intention and an open heart.

I founded the On Purpose Woman Global Community in 2000 to provide opportunities for women to create the connections they craved. I wasn't using words like connection, craving, and community back then. All I knew was that I wanted to bring women together. So, I threw a party at my home. More than 60 women showed up for that first gathering. I called it a Girlfriend Party and hosted three more that year.

Several meaningful things happened during those four Girlfriend Parties. One is that we interacted in a way that was foreign to me. We talked about things that mattered. We connected on a deeper and more authentic level than I had experienced. We formed business and life relationships and connected from a heart space. It flowed beautifully.

I had an aha moment during that first party. I understood this is how women naturally network and connect when there aren't any rules. I called it "Networking Woman Style." OPWGC was born.

Twenty-three years later, I continue to provide opportunities for women to come together in community; the richness it has brought to my life is immeasurable. I discovered that deep connection is one of my core values. I strive to connect with authenticity, openness, and curiosity. This means being real and approaching others with acceptance, listening to them, and becoming aware of their needs.

## RELATIONSHIP WITH SELF IS PRIMARY

I also discovered I had inner work to do to attract and foster the desired connections. That began a lifelong journey of healing my relationship with Self. All outer relationships reflect the relationship with the inner Self. To have deep, healthy connections, we must get that relationship right.

## WHY AUTHENTIC CONNECTION MATTERS

- Authentic connection gives you a sense of fulfillment that money, work, and material possessions can't.

- Authentic connection boosts your creativity. I prefer to work in solitude and find that's the best way to create. But I also need a genuine conversation with another to expand on my ideas. I usually come away excited by new possibilities.
- Authentic connection creates opportunities for collaboration. You must be present and engaged to notice when they appear and feel right.

## AUTHENTIC CONNECTION CREATES AUTHENTIC COMMUNITY

While you can create authentic connections one on one, you can also do it in community. Community is central to the human experience. Being part of an engaging community gives you a sense of belonging. It enables you to share yourself and support the growth of another.

A community can be anything from a physical space where people connect geographically or a virtual space such as social media groups or Zoom-like platforms. Communities bring like-minded people together with similar characteristics and shared interests.

A sense of community happens when people feel they matter to one another and have a shared faith that their needs will be met through commitment and togetherness. Being part of an authentic community can feel like being part of something greater than yourself.

A strong sense of community can also strengthen individual connections, which is a bonus.

Finding at least one community that provides some of the above is essential for a spiritual entrepreneur. Also, consider whether creating a community might enhance your work and reach.

# THE TOOL

*The Celestine Prophecy* by James Redfield came out in 1993. There are nine insights, and they are illustrated through a story. While the story could've been better written, the nine insights are brilliant. The first insight has stayed with me all these years. It is a cornerstone of my philosophy for creating connections that matter.

## THE FIRST INSIGHT

In part, the first insight reads, "I don't think that anything happens by coincidence. No one is here by accident. Everyone who crosses our path has a message for us. Otherwise, they would have taken another path or left earlier or later. The fact that these people are here means they're in our lives for some reason."

Since that first On Purpose Woman meeting in 2000, I've encouraged women at my gatherings to take notice of the woman across from them. There is a reason why she is there. If it feels right:

- Give her your attention.
- Be fully present for her.
- Listen to her.
- Ask her questions about herself and her dreams.
- Think of a way you can help her get what she needs.
- Sing her praises to other women.

Sometimes it's apparent why someone has crossed your path. Often, it isn't. Trust that everyone is bringing you something, even if it's uncomfortable or painful. Your honed discernment tells you who gets to stay after you receive the gift.

## CURIOSITY IS A SUPERPOWER WHEN IT COMES TO CONNECTING

**Be open to seemingly random meetings with others.** Be curious about why this person has crossed your path. You may never know, or you might see why years after.

**Be open to who the other person is.** Try to let go of expectations. Explore and be curious about who they are without knowing what you'll find.

**Be open to what happens.** Let go of any agenda and be curious about where the conversation might lead.

**Be open about yourself.** Suppose you try to connect with someone from your inauthentic self, and they respond positively. In that case, it means that's who they want to be in relationship with. If you move forward with the connection, you must be inauthentic to sustain it. Be curious about how this new connection will respond to the real you.

## THOUGHTS AND QUESTIONS TO PONDER

- Business relationships become most valuable when you reach the trusting stage. This takes time and requires your attention. Ask: What is one thing I can do today to increase trust with another?
- Regardless of what it says, "out there," networking is not a numbers game. It's not a game at all. It's an opportunity to enhance your life experience. Before attending an event, ask: What is my intention for showing up? What do I plan to give, and what do I most want to receive?
- You sell not only what you create but also who you are. Know who you are and why it matters. Ask: How can I express what I offer as an extension of myself?
- Help people see and feel what you do. Don't just tell them; show them. Ask: How can I best show my heart while discussing my work?
- Your network is created conversation by conversation, exchange by exchange. Make each one count. Ask: How can I be fully present and engaged in my next conversation?
- Always give without remembering. Always receive without forgetting. No scorekeeping. Ask: How can I stay grateful for the giving and the receiving?
- Your network is constantly evolving, and so are you. Ask: Is my current network meeting my needs, or is it time to move on?
- Listen generously. It's a beautiful gift to the speaker. Ask: How can I be fully present in my next encounter?

- You can't buy a network. Paying your dues does not create a community or make you part of one. Show up so others can experience your greatness. Ask: How can I be more involved and engaged with my community and supportive of the women in my network?

## TWO INVITATIONS

Take my "Are You Ready for the Spotlight?" Quiz: https://opwgc.com/spotlight/

Reach out if you feel stuck or have questions about networking with heart. Email ginnyrobertsonopw@gmail.com. Suppose you want to create some connections that matter. In that case, I invite you to attend one of my online Zoom gatherings or an in-person in Columbia, Maryland, Richmond, Virginia, or Tallahassee, Florida. Go here for the details: https://opwgc.com.

Check out the end of the book for more invitations to connect.

**Ginny Robertson** *Connects Women Around the World to Their Gifts, Their Purpose & Each Other.* She supports women with opportunities for deep connection, more visibility, and being comfortable playing a more significant role on the planet. She shines a light on and supports women in being seen and heard, creating opportunities for them to share their gifts and make a unique difference.

Ginny offers these opportunities in three ways:

On Purpose Woman Global Community - Founded in 2000, she held in-person gatherings in Maryland and Virginia. In 2020, because of covid, she took everything online and created a global community. She invites all women who yearn for deeper connection and more visibility to try one of our many free monthly online gatherings. There are also in-person gatherings in Maryland, Virginia, and Florida.

On Purpose Woman Online Magazine - Founded in 2003, On Purpose Woman Magazine was a free print magazine for 12 years. After taking a break, Ginny shifted to an online magazine accessible to everyone. It's a perfect place for women to find information and resources for their mind, body, spirit, and business.

Real Women Real Purpose Talk Show - Ginny is the co-host, and she talks with women living on purpose, sharing their gifts, and making their unique difference.

Ginny is an inspirational speaker, workshop facilitator, and author and was the co-host of the WomanTalk Live radio show on WCBM in Baltimore. In 2012, she was named one of Maryland's Top 100 Women by The Daily Record, Maryland's premier business, law, and government newspaper.

Ginny lives in Maryland with her soulmate, Don. She loves live music, especially classic rock, the ocean, the mountains, and deep connections.

https://www.opwgc.com

https://www.youtube.com/c/OnPurposeWomanGlobalCommunity

ginnyrobertsonopw@gmail.com

> *Networking with heart is focusing on what you have to offer the person across from you, not what you can get from them. It's having the courage to show up authentically and being genuinely interested in others.*
>
> ~ Ginny Robertson

CHAPTER 2

# CLARIFY WHAT YOU WANT

## HOW TO ATTRACT CLIENTS AND GROW YOUR DIVINELY INSPIRED BUSINESS

Kathryn Yarborough

## MY STORY

*I need more people to sign up or I'm going to have to quit,* I thought. *I don't know what to do.*

This wasn't the first time I felt this way, but it's the most recent. I was struggling to fill my speaker spots for my first summit. Though divinely inspired, I still faced challenges birthing it.

A few months ago, I went on an inner journey to meet with my future on-purpose self.

My eyes were closed. My breath was deep and slow. The forward movement of purpose, like an energetic moving sidewalk, propelled me toward my future on-purpose self. I met with her. She showed me that by aligning my actions with the unfolding of all of existence, in my future, I could be her—living an amazing, joy-filled, abundant life.

I asked her, "What do I need to do next to become you?"

She replied, "Grow your email list and following."

My chest tightened. Though it sounded like blah advice a business coach would give me, I felt the rightness of this task and how it would move me forward out of my comfort zone. With this task, she confirmed that I was finally ready to expand my reach and make the difference I'm here to make.

I created a goal to grow my email list to over 10,000 good contacts (coaches, healers, and on-purpose solopreneurs). Starting at 1,660 contacts, I had a long way to go.

Within a week, I heard someone say, "One of the best ways to grow an email list is to host a summit." It felt like Divine guidance. I'd participated in several summits over the past decade. Some were good experiences. Others made no impact on my life or business. At worst, some were uncomfortable because of the lack of experience, either of the organizer or the speakers, or both.

At the time I heard the suggestion to host a summit, I was getting ready to be a guest on a new type of summit. This new summit was different from traditional online summits, and I was curious about it. When it was over, I thought, *that experience was great.* I had fun, met new people, and even enrolled a new client from it. After having a positive experience, I was curious about this new format.

Within a week, as I was scrolling through my email, an invitation for a free training on hosting summits popped out at me. *This is another sign.* I went to the training and learned why this new approach was working. It all made sense to me, and I decided to go for it and host my first summit!

I birthed a win-win-win vision for the Love Your Business Summit. I believed it would be easy to fill the twenty-five speaker spots. I told people about this speaking opportunity at networking events, in my emails, and on Facebook. I even sent personal messages to several people. My calendar filled with over fifteen interviews.

But not all of these people were a right fit. I was looking for entrepreneurs who also served women coaches, healers, and on-purpose solopreneurs – not the general population. So, with only ten days left to fill my speaker spots, my chest sunk in as I looked at my list of confirmed speakers. Only twelve people were a yes. I needed twenty-five to have a successful event.

*Should I quit?* I wondered. *I could do the summit as a one-day event instead of two, but it wouldn't work as well for me or my speakers. Nothing I do works.*

My mood plummeted. My body froze. I only had ten days to fill these spots or decide to give up.

The next day I asked myself, *Kathryn, what do you really want?*

The desire to fill those speaker spots rose up from my belly. I wanted my Love Your Business Summit to be a success. I wanted to do all I could to fill those spots. And I wanted it to be easy to fill them.

After clarifying what I wanted, I was divinely inspired to reach out to the people in my Vibrant Entrepreneurs Facebook group for whom the speaking opportunity would be a good fit.

In a direct message, I wrote, "Hi Gail! Do you know that I have a few speaker spots available for my Love Your Business Summit that's happening May 19-20? If you're looking for summit speaking opportunities, let's see if it's a good fit."

Gail replied immediately, "Thank you so much! That's perfect timing for me."

When Gail and I talked, she decided to be a sponsor for the summit and got two speaker spots. Many others responded and scheduled a chat with me. Most of those beautiful souls said *yes!* I invited another speaker to be a sponsor and receive two speaker spots. I gave myself two speaker spots.

Within ten days, all the summit speaker spots were filled. Joy bubbled up through my belly and chest. *I get to host the Love Your Business Summit!*

We entrepreneurs all need clients, right?! Whether you call them clients, customers, members, registrants, attendees, students, writers, or something else like speakers, we all need them.

Without clients, you can't do the work you're called to do; you won't feel the amazing sense of satisfaction and fulfillment that comes with making a difference in someone's life and generating an abundant life-sustaining income from your business. It's impossible without clients.

What do you need to do to attract more clients?

# THE TOOL

I teach five steps to grow an on-purpose business that will lead you to having all the clients you want. You can read more about these steps in my book, *KEEP MOVING FORWARD: A Guide for the On Purpose Solopreneur*. Here's a short summary:

1. Have a vision for the future that excites you. Keep it front of mind.
2. Create a plan to manifest that vision. Craft sellable offers based on what your ideal clients want and design a client-focused marketing plan to reach your ideal clients.
3. Talk to yourself positively. Be encouraging and forward-looking.
4. Take action and learn from your experiences. You have to do stuff to attract clients.
5. Clear your blocks and inner resistances. It's on you to declutter the old thoughts and beliefs that no longer serve.

However, the bottom line is that if you want more clients, you'll attract them. If you don't want clients, you won't attract them.

So, do you want more clients?

The answer should be an easy and resounding YES. But it's often more like a yeah, maybe, probably, I think I want them, but. Here are some of the "yeah buts" I've heard from clients.

Yeah, but…

- I do everything everybody tells me to do, but nothing's working.
- My kids are going through a rough patch, and they need me more than ever.
- Only a few people came to my webinar, and no one signed up for my offer.
- I'm not comfortable on social media.
- No one signs up through my website.
- I've paid a lot of money for a coaching program, but I didn't get any clients.
- Other people are attracting clients, but I'm not.

# CLARIFY WHAT YOU WANT | 15

- I don't have time for many clients because I still have to work full-time to pay the bills.

Get honest with yourself. If you can relate to some of those "yeah buts," I ask again, do you really want clients?

If you're not sure, on the fence, or swirling in negativity or ambivalence, I recommend that you use my tool. It will help you clarify what you want and then manifest it. However, if your answer is a resounding yes, go to my website and grab my free Client Ready Assessment. After completing it, you'll know what you need to do to become a magnet to your ideal clients.

Use this tool to shift out of negativity, clarify what you really want, and start moving forward. Though you can use this tool for any aspect of life, I recommend, in this case, using it with a focus on attracting clients.

## STEP ONE

Get out some paper. At the top of one sheet, write "I don't want..." At the top of another, write, "What I do want is..."

## STEP TWO

Complete your I DON'T WANT list. Fill it in with all the negative thoughts that arise when you think about attracting clients. Here's my example regarding attracting attendees to my upcoming Love Your Business Summit.

I don't want...

- It to be hard to get people to register for the summit.
- A low number of people to register for the summit.
- People to think, there are so many summits out there—why should I sign up for this one?
- People who register to have a bad or negative experience.
- Attendees to NOT upgrade to VIP.
- The speakers to not do their part to enroll attendees for the summit.

I encourage you to make your I DON'T WANT list as comprehensive as possible.

## STEP THREE

Say the following sentence completion out loud for each item on your I DON'T WANT list, and write the second part of the sentence completion as a bullet point for your WHAT I DO WANT list.

If I don't want _____, what I do want is _____ .

Saying this out loud is more powerful than if you just write down the opposite of what you don't want. Your response will come from your whole self—your body, heart, mind, and Higher-self—not just your head. If the wording is messy and grammatically incorrect, that's fine. You'll clean it up later.

Here's my example for the first bullet point.

If I don't want (it to be hard to get people to register for the summit), what I do want is (for lots of people to want to register for the summit and to feel good about it).

Do that for every item on your don't want list. Here's my example:

What I do want is…

- for lots of people to want to register for the summit and to feel good about it.
- for over 500 people to register for the summit. It would be awesome if over 1000 people registered for it!
- for people to think, this sounds like a great summit. I'm going to it!
- for the people who register to be the right people for this summit. For them to enjoy it and get a lot out of the experience.
- over 50% of the people who register to upgrade to VIP.
- for the speakers to have fun enrolling people into the summit and for them to feel good about their experience successfully attracting 25 or more attendees for this summit!

## STEP FOUR

Edit your WHAT I DO WANT list so it's an "I WANT" list, and when you read it, all the words should make sense and feel good. Read it over and add anything else you want.

Here's my example.

I want...

- lots of people to feel good about the summit and register for it.
- over 1000 coaches, healers, and on-purpose solopreneurs to register for the summit!
- people to think this sounds like a great summit, when they visit the landing page and then to register for it.
- people who register for the summit to be the right people for this summit – people who will enjoy it and get a lot out of their experience at it.
- over 50% of the people who register to upgrade to VIP.
- the speakers to have fun enrolling people into the summit and for them to feel good about their experience successfully attracting over 25 summit attendees!
- the attendees to have an easy time accessing the summit, and over 10% of them to attend each live presentation.

## STEP FIVE

Throw away your DON'T WANT list. You don't ever need to look at it again! Read over your I WANT list. It should feel great. If it doesn't, use the don't want/do want sentence completion process until your I WANT list feels wonderful to you.

## STEP SIX

Once you know what you want, you get to activate the Law of Attraction by writing a new story about the future as if it's happening now. Choose one item on your I WANT list and turn it into a prompt for your new story by making it an affirmation and adding, "and this means. . ."

For my example, I'm going to use the second item on my list. My prompt looks like this: Over 1000 coaches, healers, and on-purpose solopreneurs register for the Love Your Business summit, and this means. . .

Put your prompt at the top of a piece of paper, then complete the sentence as many times as you want. I like to write my new story in bullet form, but you can just as easily write paragraphs. Write it in the present tense (not the future). In other words, if, when you read it over, you find things like "I'll be making more money," change them to "I make more money."

Fill in the blank with as many items that come to mind. Then, as you imagine it happening, add feelings, sounds, sights, and any other sensory experiences that will make your new story feel more real.

Here's my example.

Over 1000 coaches, healers, and on-purpose solopreneurs register for the Love Your Business summit, and this means:

- People want to attend it.
- Everyone shares it. I share it. The speakers share it. And people who register for it share it.
- Every day through May 19, I see registrations in my inbox - some days it's over 100 emails!
- When I look in my email list on May 19, I see over 1000 people in the Love Your Business Summit list.
- The Love Your Business Summit has great energy. I keep feeling positive about it!

After clarifying what you want and writing a new story to manifest it, follow the Divine guidance you receive. If you're wondering what to do to attract more clients, take my Client Ready Assessment. It's a free resource on my website. Once you complete it, you'll have five action steps that will move you forward in manifesting more clients.

**Kathryn Yarborough** is a manifesting clients mentor and vibrant speaker coach for women coaches, healers, and on-purpose solopreneurs. She teaches her clients how to manifest clients, be authentically vibrant, and grow a business they love. She's the founder of the Manifesting Clients Academy, the creator of the Vibrant Entrepreneurs Circle, an Amazon best-selling author, and an inspirational speaker. She runs a great Facebook group called Vibrant Entrepreneurs, where you'll find tips on attracting clients and opportunities to connect with other cool solopreneurs.

As a thriving on-purpose solopreneur for over 22 years, she uses her knowledge and experience to support her clients on their entrepreneurial journeys. She launched her private practice in 2001 as a dance/movement therapist, then added manifestation coaching and integrative breathwork to her toolbox. In 2017, she committed to working solely with solopreneurs and now provides training, community, and opportunities for visibility. She's a leader and speaker in the On Purpose Woman Global Community, the past owner of the Center for Embodied Consciousness, and a past President of Omni Toastmasters.

Kathryn's a divorced (and happily single) mom of a cool adult son. She likes to journal, walk, do conscious breathwork, swim, and watch action-adventure movies. She lives in central Florida.

Connect with her on the following sites:

Website:
https://www.manifestingclientsacademy.com/

Facebook group:
https://www.facebook.com/groups/vibrantentrepreneurslovelife

CHAPTER 3

# THE WRITE CONNECTION WITH SPIRIT

## HOW TO CHANNEL AND SHARE WORDS THAT GROW YOUR BUSINESS

Laura Di Franco, MPT, Publisher

## MY STORY

*I think I just channeled that.*

Even after two decades as a healer, I still didn't have the authentic connection to Source that I was craving and envied in my peers. They seemed to have this magical energy that appeared from some mysterious place I didn't seem to be able to connect to.

*That must be only for special kinds of healers.*

But on this particular day, something shifted. And it was powerful. I knew the words came from a place much bigger than me and weren't meant for only me.

Channeling words from a place bigger than you (give that source your favorite name) isn't only for certain people—it's for everyone. It's for you. You can channel brave words that come from that magical, much-bigger place and build your business. In fact, the words that move through from that connection are much more apt to build your business than any you've learned to write through some copywriting course you took.

I'm not new to magical moments. As a healer with 30 years of holistic and alternative training, I knew to look for the signs, and I saw them regularly. But I craved more than anything to hear the messages in a louder, more straightforward way. That was the ability I doubted I had.

In 2014, I signed up for Quantum Leap (an advanced John F. Barnes Myofascial Release course) and immediately felt the energy shift. Interesting things started happening. I usually booked a hotel room alone, but something in me decided to reach out to the online community: "Anyone up for sharing a room in Sedona?" One of my colleagues answered that request, and I was set to meet Ronda at the Phoenix airport car rental hub.

The journey to Dulles Airport that morning was smooth. The Uber was on time, as was the flight, and when I boarded and headed to the rear of the plane, I saw I'd have a row of three seats to myself.

*Sigh. Yes! This is awesome!*

"Anything to drink, dear?"

"Just a water, please."

I sipped and practiced letting my body melt into the seat with a few exhales and felt the urge to grab my notebook. I pulled down the middle seat's tray, slid my cup over, folded *my* tray up, leaned down, and reached for the floor to grab my purse. I noticed the pull in my right upper traps and back. *Ugh, I'm tight,* I thought. The journal and pen I always brought on my travels beckoned. I wrote.

NOTE: The version of the poem you're about to read is a special update from its original version published in my first book of poetry, *Warrior Love, A Journal to Inspire Your Fiercely Alive Whole Self.*

## THE QUANTUM LEAP (GOD ON THE PLANE)

*The journey begins.*
*The cab is early.*
*The plane is on time.*
*Everything's done, organized, arranged, and confirmed.*
*From Dulles to Dallas to Sedona, I'm sitting by myself*
*in a row of three seats.*
*Yep. Little old me—space.*
*I'm filled with excitement and anticipation,*
*the energy of this event is building.*

*From achievement*
*to depression*
*to sad lunch*
*to joyful birthday weekend*
*in an unforgettable snow. . .*
*. . . don't think I don't feel you, Universe,*
*that push nudging me from behind,*
*crowding my space,*
*waiting for me to make a move.*

*I sit still and feel it instead.*
*I don't go to class.*
*I don't fake the lunch.*
*I listen and feel.*
*And I recognize the okayness of it all,*
*even in its dampness.*

*With a deep inhale,*
*I don't get tighter.*
*I feel and trust in you, and I'm free.*

*I realize the nudge behind me*
*was you all along.*
*Finally, I recognize you, God.*
*I've never really liked that name though.*
*So many conflicting ideas*
*about what you are.*
*Too much room for getting it wrong.*

*That's the funny part.*
*All the ideas are right.*
*How you show up for me is mine.*
*How you show up for her is hers.*
*My filter of love is purple.*
*Hers is yellow.*
*We're all looking at and feeling*
*the same thing.*

*But it looks purple from here,*
*yellow from there.*
*I like yellow.*
*I can feel yellow.*
*I can at least be open to yellow*
*because what I know is*
*we're all looking at the same thing—love.*

*My story today begins with an awakening,*
*to love and God on the plane.*
*What could matter more?*
*The story continues as the others arrive today*
*and we lift each other up*
*in healing love.*

*Red, yellow, purple,*
*orange, green, blue. . .*
*. . . we meld together*
*into one amazing, magnetic, magical rainbow.*

*This colorful force has powers,*
*superpowers!*
*It's true and real;*
*my purple self has felt it so many times*
*there's no room left for doubt.*
*To live in a space without doubt dragging you down?*
*That's freedom.*
*Quiet, powerful, colorful, super-powered freedom.*
*Once felt, it never dies.*

*So, if for a moment*
*you feel weighted down with doubt*
*you have a brief forgetting*
*and you go unconscious to love*
*no worries.*
*That freedom you know will shine through the cracks*

*and blast the darkness.*

*You won't lose your freedom.*

*You never lost it in the first place.*

*You were looking for purple*

*and maybe it was yellow that day.*

I scribbled the words you just read in my notebook fast and furiously, placed the notebook back in my purse, and enjoyed the rest of my flight.

*Hmm,* I thought. *That was interesting.* I reached for the cup of water with another long exhale.

As soon as the plane landed, I was off to meet Ronda and enjoy a conversation that was like finding a long-lost soul sister.

"OMG, we have so much in common!"

"I know! This is going to be an interesting weekend!"

The two-hour car ride flew as we discovered all the life moments we each shared—weird parallel lives happening thousands of miles from each other.

The voice started the next morning.

*That wasn't just for you. You need to read that out loud.*

Whoever was talking to me repeated the message over and over. It spoke while I got ready for our first day of the seminar, during breakfast, and as I was finding my seat in the center of the ballroom of over 200 chairs.

*That wasn't just for you. You need to read that out loud.*

Up until that point, public speaking scared the shit out of me. The visceral feeling of imminent death coursed through me any time I was to speak, even in small groups of people, and especially when I tried to stand up for myself, even with one single person. I'll sum this up: My lifelong healing journey has been about finding my voice and worth and claiming my space in the world out loud.

But that day, I wasn't so sure. When John, our instructor, took the stage, he even invited us to speak.

"Anyone have any comments or questions or anything they want to share before we begin?"

Brave soul after brave soul raised their hand to speak. I couldn't raise mine. I was too afraid.

*That wasn't just for you. You need to read that out loud.*

*OMG, okay, okay!*

The safe bet was to ask for permission. Holy fuck, how many times had I asked for permission to speak in the past? I approached John at the table on the side of the ballroom just after the break.

"Hi, John. I was wondering if I could read something I wrote to the class."

"How long is it?"

"Just a few minutes."

"Okay."

The full-body shaking started immediately and continued as everyone took their seats. After the break, John hopped on the stage and said, "Somebody wanted to share something?"

I stood up (from the center seat in the ballroom of 200 people I'd chosen that day), pulled my journal out of my purse, and read the words I journaled on the plane out loud. The shaking was so bad, but my voice did not quiver. In fact, all morning, students were asked to speak up when asking a question. My voice was loud and clear and didn't sound like my own. I read the piece from beginning to end and sat down almost before the last word escaped my lips, quickly bowing my head to avoid eye contact with anyone around me.

The room then erupted in applause. I slowly looked up from my gaze at my feet and smiled. But that wasn't the best part. After the next break, I darted for the door, again trying to avoid eye contact, when my friend Jude tapped me on the shoulder.

*Ugh, no, I don't want to talk to anyone right now.*

"Thank you so much for sharing your poem with us."

*Poem? Oh!*

"Here, I want you to have this."

She handed me a purple pen. I looked at her fully in the eyes and felt the love.

That was the day I became a poet.

I'd written many poems before that day, but after the seminar, I returned home to pen at least 50 additional poems and self-published a total of five books of poetry. Even better, I've used my poems in my business, during talks, in books, and on stage so many times that I've lost count. Every time I let the words that move through me from that much bigger place do the talking, I feel confident I'm sharing words that mean something and have a divine purpose. Words from this connection feel easy, powerful, and like the real me. Beats any copywriting course I've ever taken—and I've taken a few!

I want to show you a simple exercise to channel *your* brave words. Whether journaling, poems, or words for your business, detach from the outcome at first and just practice connecting. You can refine and craft what you want to share with others afterward.

First and foremost, I write to Feng Shui my soul. Then I decide what to share. Prioritizing your healing is a powerful way to write.

# THE TOOL

### WRITING TO FENG SHUI YOUR SOUL

Whenever I write, be it for me, my business, social media, etc., I connect first. If I forget to connect, it's very likely that the words will start to feel tight. My body constricts; I begin holding my breath, and then my mind starts with all the self-sabotaging BS.

I've learned to recognize this pattern and fine-tune my awareness practice to the point I can sit, connect, and write easily now. I trust the practice. Because this is a practice, know that it gets better and way more magical as you do more of it. When you feel amazing, like the real you is peeking from behind the curtain, that's the feeling to go for! Purpose-driven fear feels like survival fear, only it has some excitement and pizazz to it. Learn to discern between the two! Follow the purpose-driven kind of fear like a compass!

Here are some steps to take to connect to Source and allow words to flow from a much bigger place than you:

1. Set the stage by curating a sacred space to sit and write. Set up your room, desk, lighting, chair, crystals, candle—whatever helps you feel awesome—first. When you love your writing space and are vibrating higher there, the connection comes easily.
2. Gather your notebook, pen, and timer. Get comfy.
3. Take at least five minutes to breathe and meditate. Don't let the "M" word scare you. Meditation is magical. Just sit still and breathe for a few minutes, allowing all the thoughts, and notice everything you feel. Be curious. Clear your mind and focus on the sensations. No rules here. Eyes open or closed, it's up to you. Body position is also up to you. Be supported and comfortable as possible without falling asleep. And heck, if that happens, you probably need a nap more than you need to write right now!
4. The writing: Set a timer for five minutes and write as fast as you can without censoring yourself. What is the message moving through you today? Start with the prompt "I feel" and fill in the blank. Detach from all outcomes of what this is, what it's for, or anyone else reading it. This is just for you to warm up your connection and Feng Shui your inner spaces.
5. Once you complete the writing, sit back and take a couple of breaths. Now read the words out loud to yourself. Notice anything you feel. You can journal a bit about that now, too. How do you feel hearing the words?

## WRITING TO HELP OTHERS AND BUILD YOUR BUSINESS

When writing for your business, you sometimes forget that the connection is the most important part and try too hard to write the 'correct' way for everyone else.

It's the connection that creates the message that resonates more powerfully. The connection gives the energy to the words that'll attract what you want. The connection, energy, and intention are what matters when you write for the world to read!

Here are some additional steps for crafting a piece of writing for your business that will resonate with your prospective clients, and have them click on your offerings to find out more.

1. Follow steps 1-3 above.

2. The writing: For this exercise, you can craft a blog, social post, email newsletter, or whatever you want. You might at first detach from the outcome of what exactly it ends up being. You can figure that out later.

   First, ask yourself these questions:

   What matters to me right now?

   What aspect of my business turns me on the most?

   What am I passionate about sharing in terms of a crucial aspect of what I do that will help my clients solve a problem they're having?

   Start writing when an idea pops up that you're getting excited about. I want you to write the juiciest love letter to that prospective ideal client about this idea. Pretend they're sitting next to you on the couch, and you're sharing a wonderful, passionate conversation. What do you want them to know? How do you want them to feel? Write it all down as fast as you can without censoring yourself. Get it all out. Don't proof or edit as you go.

   When you've completed the writing, pause, breathe, and read it aloud. How is it making you feel? Now you can add, subtract, and self-edit as you see fit.

3. Power Editing

   Now read your piece with a few things in mind to amp up the power and help the reader know that this is for them.

   Where can you offer your authentic self here? Oh, did you skip that part? Share a vulnerable story about you that helps build some trust with your reader. It's absolutely the thing most business writing is missing. We step up into master teacher mode way too fast before the reader trusts us as a human being. Do that part first.

   Next, make sure you're talking about what you know your reader is struggling with or what their deepest desires are. Show them you understand. How can you connect with the emotion they are feeling?

   Lastly, how do you want them to feel? Make sure you're feeling it before you write it. If you're feeling tired, bored, or a little bit of not-good-enough, remember that's the energy they're feeling from your written word. Conjure up the energy you want them to feel, and then write.

4. Remember some important pieces. For my business, I try to remember some important aspects of writing that help the reader resonate and engage.

    - Write a strong hook. Make them put their phone down in the first paragraph.
    - Write clearly, with easy-to-read font, short paragraphs, headings, subheadings, and lists.
    - Create transition sentences or paragraphs that help them keep reading.
    - Don't use big words they have to look up in a dictionary. Write at a fifth-grade level.
    - Make sure you give the reader a call to action.

5. Move through your fear and share. I often share unedited writing on social media, especially when it's a poem. I just don't care anymore about the mistakes. It's more important that someone read and be helped than getting it perfect. When I go to publish, I spend more time editing and proofing. But even then, it can be paralyzing if you focus too much on perfection. My advice is to share stuff. And then share more stuff. Share until the shaking dies down and the confidence rolls in, and you're basking in the light of changing the world with your brave words.

    So now that you're connecting, writing, and sharing with the world, what's your next step? Is it time to write your book? Land that column in a magazine? Start your blog? Whatever it is, and whatever kind of words you're planning on crafting next, remember that connection, energy, and intention is the key to it all. Practice prioritizing the connection to Spirit, and the words will come.

One final note of inspiration, writers. It's all been said, done, and written before—but not by you. Someone out there is waiting to read your message in exactly the unique way only you can share it. Your divine connection and spirit are what make those words unique. Your words change the world when you're brave enough to share them. It's time to be brave.

**Laura Di Franco,** CEO of Brave Healer Productions, is an award-winning publisher specializing in business strategy for holistic health and wellness professionals ready to become bestselling authors. She has 30 years of expertise in holistic physical therapy, 14 years of training in martial arts, and her company has published over 55 Amazon bestselling books.

The community is over 1000 authors strong, and the mission is to wake the world up to what's possible. Join us on Facebook in the Brave Badass Healers, a Community for World-Changers group to enjoy free monthly business development and networking. Want some advice about your book idea? Schedule a chat with our publishing team!

Laura is a divorced mom (of two adult kids and one dog), lover of the sunrise and dark chocolate, spoken-word poet, inspirational speaker, and is convinced she was a race car driver in a past life. She has a contagious passion for helping you share brave words that build your business and leave your legacy. BraveHealer.com

Connect with Laura:

https://LauraDiFranco.com

https://www.Facebook.com/BraveHealerbyLaura/

https://www.Instagram.com/BraveHealerProductions

https://www.linkedin.com/in/laura-di-franco-mpt-1b037a5/

https://www.youtube.com/c/BraveHealerProductionswithLauraDiFranco

CHAPTER 4

# THE CRISPY YOGI

## BATTLING BURNOUT, GRIEF, AND INJURY

Pat Perrier, MA, MBA, E-RYT 500

*Often the most unexpected, unpredictable moments in life are the ones that leave the biggest impression and that teach us to roll with the punches.*

~ Natalya Neidhart

## MY STORY

"I'll just do the Butterfly sequence again. I've practically got it memorized, and they won't care."

"I can do the forward bend sequence again. They won't care."

"I know it's the flow class, but they won't care if I toss in a restorative practice."

But it wasn't "they" who didn't care. It was me.

And I was afraid that my students could tell. It was a combination of several things: the post-Covid reality of smaller class sizes, an ocean of unresolved grief, and the fact that I was facing my own pretty intense injury, which not only impacted my own practice but my ability to move forward with a program near and dear to my heart: prenatal yoga. And—quite frankly—burnout.

I've been a yoga teacher since 2014 and have been a studio owner since 2015, including the "Covid Times," where our entire state was shut down, and we had to immediately pivot from in-studio classes to online. We first went to Facebook Live and "pay when you watch," which was a total crap shoot, then registering for Zoom classes with monthly billing for classes till we could open back up.

We invested in the systems to support the "new way of doing things" and trained teachers on technology they weren't really comfortable with. We learned to teach when we really couldn't interact in-person with our students. It was indeed a new world.

Anyway, we managed to survive till we could open up again, one of the few studios in the area which did hang on. And students have come back, slowly in some cases.

But I noticed a change in myself as a teacher and a yoga practitioner. I wasn't motivated. I wasn't putting a lot of time into creating new and exciting sequences. I was going through the motions. And the fact that over that time, my left hip was getting worse wasn't helping.

I was getting irritated all the time. All. The. Time. I was aggravated about subbing for a teacher. I was annoyed when things didn't go to plan (and I'm old enough to know about plans). I was irritated when I had to teach. I was mad at my body because it wasn't cooperating. I was incensed that students weren't coming back at the rate I thought they should. When I couldn't find a sequence I wanted, I was internally screaming at myself for my own disorganization. When I needed a sub and couldn't get one, I was seething, telling myself: *All this subbing that I'm doing, and when I need one? Bupkis!*

I was shoving all of this down, plastering a smile on my face and literally clenching my jaw at the pain, grief, and exhaustion I felt. I thought I was hiding it well.

On top of dealing with the loss of my dear (and only) sister, there were some physical things happening that I just couldn't wrap my mind around. *I mean, I did all the right things: exercised, ate well, and got enough rest. I thought I was taking care of my body. My body apparently has other ideas.* Between the drastic effects of grief, which I was "going to deal with soon," and the long-term effects of living in a hyper-mobile body, something had to give. And give it did, spectacularly, if I may say so.

I was diagnosed a year ago with two tears in my hip labrum, bone spurs on both the acetabulum (socket) and the femoral head, and advanced osteoarthritis. I tried everything. A hip brace, red light therapy, ice, yoga therapy, cortisone shots, PRP treatment, heat, and physical therapy. I modified my own practice to adapt to the injuries. I knew there was really nothing stopping the arthritis. I was on a mission to stave off the worst of the damage and keep on keeping on until it was inevitable that stronger measures needed to be taken. I was told that a hip replacement was "on the horizon," but I didn't realize that the metaphorical horizon was closer than I thought it would be. I thought I was doing what needed to be done; I went faithfully to the therapist and made sure that I balanced the "do the things" and the "rest a bit," which can be complex. You don't want to do too much, but you don't want to do too little. It's a dance with the bone devils. Do too much, and you pay for it. Do too little, and you pay for it.

Within that year, I went from a little limp to full-on using a cane. My gait is awful, I feel like Tim Conway (if you're in your 30s, Google him), and my normal 24-inch stride is a shuffle. This has, of course, affected my knees, back, right shoulder, elbow (due to cane usage), right hand, and feet. I'm also bent over, unable to straighten up because the muscles around my hip have tightened up to protect it. I sound like a popcorn machine crossed with the percussion section of a marching band when I walk, and aside from the noise, it's starting to be painful and sometimes feels as if my leg won't support me. Tennessee Ernie Ford (Google again, folks) would say I have "a hitch in my git-along." My 85-year-old mother, who had her hip replaced last fall, is running rings around me.

My "doing the things" circle was pretty wide. I taught yoga three days a week; I subbed when I was asked; I volunteered at a therapeutic riding center cleaning out stalls (shoveling horse manure is indeed meditative and gives you room to sort out your thoughts). Proofreading books and manuscripts. Gardening and biking. Going with family and friends on jaunts and lunch dates. Very active in my church. That circle shrank swiftly and inexorably.

Currently, I'm teaching out of a chair because my mobility has been severely impacted. On a positive note, my verbal cues are incredibly improved, and I've finally learned how to mirror! On the negative side, I feel like the energy I'm projecting to the class isn't where it was pre-Covid (or "pre-plague" as I like to call it). I thought, perhaps naively, that people would be anxious to come back to in-person classes, and we'd have numbers like we used to. That didn't happen. Classes that were full were now sparse. At one point, we weren't even able to have workshops or private sessions.

What's a studio owner to do? Well, I did panic. I worried about whether we'd survive this. I saw the impact of Covid on the small businesses in our community, and I was scared witless that we'd be "another number in the column" of those who succumbed to the virus. But we wouldn't close during the pandemic. We'd be among the ones who just couldn't make the come-back. It kept me up at night, along with the pain and stiffness in my body and the unresolved grief in my heart.

Now, in the post-Covid environment, we've brought back workshops, the safety mandates have lifted, and we see an increase in some of the classes to the "before" levels.

And it became time to address my own feelings of burnout. But how? I know, go ahead and laugh. I'm a yoga teacher. I teach the tools to address stress and anxiety. I teach people how to manage the monkey mind and calm the nervous system. I did a literal raft of videos teaching guided meditation, pranayama, and easily-accessible poses to help turn down the noise. *So why can't those tools work for me? Or, why aren't the tools working for me?*

# THE TOOL

I'm a Capricorn. I'm extremely practical and a doer. I needed to find a tool that helped me focus my attention on getting my creativity back. And I needed to address the elephant in the room: my hip was worsening; despite doing what I was supposed to, it wasn't working. It was working according to the plan of the Universe, not the plan I had mapped out in my head. All the manifestation in the world wouldn't stop the inescapable worsening of osteoarthritis.

First, I addressed my concerns with my orthopedic doctor, and we made some decisions about care. It is what it is, and I needed to know where I was going with this. I needed assurance that I'd have quality of life, I'd be able to sleep through the night, and awake refreshed rather than in pain and exhausted. I wanted to cuddle my new baby grandniece; I wanted to go back to shoveling manure. I wanted to revive my prenatal program. I wanted to teach workshops again. I wanted that circle of "do the things" to expand to close to where it was before. I was in a vicious circle of "do too much and pay for it" and "do too little and pay for it." Screwed either way, ya know?

Once that was taken care of, I had to apply all the tools I knew to get my yoga mojo back, and I had to start revisiting the tools I learned in graduate school about systems and processes.

I'm a notebook kinda gal. I write out my sequences because I like to have that order in front of me. I have never been one to memorize a sequence because it didn't feel authentic to me. If you're a teacher who can do that, I applaud you! I've had the privilege of being taught by teachers who are expert at this. It's just not me; I have learned that over the years. As an experienced yoga teacher, I have, of course, tossed a sequence when I've had to re-engineer it on the fly, depending on who shows up. Our demographic ranges from the mid-30s to the mid-80s, and that can be just one class!

So, sometimes, I have a class on forward bends planned, but a couple of students walk in who I know have conditions that aren't conducive to a lot of forward bending. Plot twist! My notebooks came in handy, but they were disorganized. I would often take out a sequence (binders are also my BFFs), and instead of putting it back where it was supposed to go, I shoved it in the backpack I kept in the studio for everyone to use.

I took a few days and spread everything out in front of me. I organized the sequences by the peak poses and themes and began re-writing sequences where the cues had become out of date.

Taking time for myself to do online training also helped. I learned about new science and new ways of adapting the pose to the body instead of the other way around.

Here are some tips you might find helpful.

- **Always keep learning.** This seems obvious, right? But sometimes, as a business owner, you get stuck in your rut. You think that you don't have time. You don't have time to *not* train. Keep current in your profession.
- **Make your systems work for you.** You don't let the system run you. There are all kinds of things out there that are new and shiny, as well as tried and true. And they might work. It's really easy to be attracted

to the fancy stuff. You want your system to be something you can actually almost naturally integrate. Not something where there's a steep learning curve and the system requires more energy than you may want to put into it. This system may exist out there somewhere, but you may also develop your own. Make sure that whatever system you employ, you're consistent in its implementation.

- **Reevaluate your expectations.** What do you expect of yourself? As a studio owner, what do you expect of your teachers? What have you "always done" that may need to be ditched or revised? Are you flexible enough to look honestly at your processes and see where you are and where you want to be?
- **Call a coach.** Coaches are a great way to touch base with yourself. Reach out to your network and see if there are recommendations. You can usually at least have an introductory chat to see if you click.
- **Take time to do what brings you joy.** It may mean spending time in nature, getting a massage, journaling, art—do something that takes you out of your own head and away from the business. Reenergize. You and your teachers and students will thank you for it.
- **Ask for help.** Maybe this should have been the first one.

I had a hard time asking for help. I was determined to keep moving. I was determined to pull myself up by my own bootstraps. My ego got in the way of my body.

I finally (!) started allowing my students to help me. *"Lisa, can you grab the screen and put it in front of the door?" "Dee, can you close the prop room door?"* Thanking them for their willingness to help and acknowledging that they are gracing me with this blessing has been an eye-opener. They want to help. They feel heavily invested in the classes I teach and are part of the reason the studio is still here.

I also changed the way I end the class. I've been fortunate to be able to implement something and inevitably have students say, "Wow! I really needed that!" when, in truth, I did it for myself.

At the end of the class, as we sit with our hands in Anjali Mudra, I invite the students to send gratitude to their physical body. *"For the things your beautiful body does that you don't have to think about, for the things this body does when you ask it to, and for the fact that this body carries the wonder-filled light that is the essence of you."* I pause. I let those words sink into each of us. As I sit with those words as well, I start to feel a glimmer. Ever-so-slightly, I feel the warmth of that light start to spark just a tiny bit more than it did the last time I uttered those phrases.

Maybe. Just maybe, the energy and power of these words will eventually cool the lingering brushfire of burnout and bring back the joy that I once felt when doing the thing that I feel called to do: teaching. Inspiring. Being unabashedly me and feeling the resonance in the studio when the students feel unabashedly themselves. When that energy comes together, we all feel it. And the world is a better place for it.

**Pat Perrier,** MA, MBA, E-RYT 500, is a yoga studio owner and teacher. She is a Liberal Arts graduate, with a varied career background, from corporate to legal, to education, to non-profits, with a side of newspaper columnist and reporter. She enjoys writing and editing, having an eagle eye for misspellings and sentence construction.

As a yoga teacher, her philosophy is, "Come as you are." She helps students create a practice that fits their bodies. She loves to teach beginners, and her forte is coming up with innovative ways to make a yoga practice fun, as well as helping students find their own alignment in the poses.

She has owned and operated Just Breathe Yoga Studio in Crest Hill, Illinois, since 2015 and has been a yoga teacher since 2014. She is certified in Yoga for Healthy Aging and prenatal yoga. She has her 200 and 500-hour yoga certifications in Iyengar-based alignment principles, with an emphasis on adapting the pose to the student, not the other way around.

She is a thrice-published author with Brave Healer Productions, including *The Ultimate Guide to Self-Healing, Volume 3* and *Volume 5,* and *Whole-Hearted Wonder Women 50-Plus.* All of these are Amazon International Bestsellers. She also works with authors helping shape and polish their thoughts into words.

In her spare time, she enjoys volunteering at an equine therapy stable, knitting, gardening, riding her bike, and reading murder mysteries. She also enjoys cooking, baking, and reading cookbooks. She looks forward to life after a hip replacement.

Connect with Pat:

www.just-breatheyoga.com

info@just-breatheyoga.com

https://www.facebook.com/yogapatperrier/

CHAPTER 5

# PUT YOURSELF FIRST

## UNLOCKING PASSION, PLEASURE, AND DESIRES BY FOCUSING ON YOURSELF

Tamara Robinson, Sex & Intimacy Coach

The trauma of suffering a miscarriage caused me to feel hurt, pain, and disconnected from my body. I felt broken and undesirable after my ten-year marriage ended in divorce. I never allowed myself to process or feel these feelings, but eventually, I decided to take some time to look within. I needed to focus on myself and, more importantly, not feel guilty.

Are you tired of putting the needs of others before your own?

Well, let's flip the script. It's time to put the focus on your needs and desires and feel good about it.

When thinking about your life, chances are you've spent time putting the needs of others before your own. But what if I told you that you could enjoy a new level of joy and fulfillment by putting yourself first? As we age, we often become more focused on others and less on ourselves. But by prioritizing your own needs and desires, you can tap into a wellspring of passion and pleasure you never knew existed.

When you tap into the source of passion and pleasure, you may feel more engaged and fulfilled professionally and personally.

Regarding professional success, connecting with your pleasure and desires unlocks the purpose and motivation that fuels your entrepreneurial spirit. This is important when your business is created from your personal experience. Connecting with your passion, pleasure, and intimate desires allows you to be more relatable, especially when you are guiding or coaching clients on a similar path that you've traveled.

Passion and pleasure inspire you to take risks, push past obstacles, and create in a way that sets your business apart. When fully aligned with your values and vision, you can make decisions and take action more confidently and clearly, which can benefit your business.

On a personal level, prioritizing your needs and desires can increase happiness. You may feel more comfortable expressing yourself authentically and creating deeper connections with others, which improves relationships with friends, family, and loved ones.

# MY STORY

As a divorced single mom, I sometimes felt guilty about pursuing the dreams and goals I placed on the back burner. I put all my time, energy, and focus on my daughter, family, work, and home. My focus was outside of who I was, and I neglected myself because I thought that was normal and the right thing to do as a woman and a mom.

"I don't have time" was something I said a lot.

With a long list of priorities and tasks to accomplish every day, I often felt busy and overwhelmed with life. Days passed by when I placed others (family, household responsibilities, work, etc.) higher on my priority list. Self-care was at the end of my list; honestly, it often wasn't a priority at all. I desired more time for myself but felt guilty about prioritizing my needs, asking for help, or even taking a mental health break. I needed self-care but didn't quite understand what it was. I didn't know how to enjoy pleasure. I didn't know what made me feel good.

*Is it supposed to be this hard? I want to stay in bed all day and hide under the covers!*

I felt drained from life and soon realized something was missing. I couldn't meet my needs and desires because my focus was outside myself. Eventually, I found time to register for an online meditation course. It was a 30-day journey of self-discovery using mantras, journal prompts, and meditation tips.

*Zen mode re-activated!*

After practicing meditation for a while, I reconnected with my love of dance in a unique way. I signed up for pole dance fitness classes at a local dance studio for women. Dance has always been my first love since childhood, but I put my passion for dance on hold to focus on other things I felt were more important.

*...because that's what good moms do. Right?*

Once I understood the importance of self-care and reconnecting with my passions, I scheduled my dance classes between the drop-off and pick-up times of my daughter's ballet classes. While she had fun at the ballet studio, I enjoyed my pole fitness and chair dance classes! We were winning!

*Yes! I feel so alive and free in these dance classes!*

While practicing meditation and enjoying my pole fitness classes, I read a book on female sexuality and orgasm. I began to study the connection between meditation and sexuality as a wellness practice to understand myself better. At this time, I uncovered some unhealed trauma I needed to give gentle attention to. This unhealed trauma kept me from enjoying the pleasure and intimacy I craved and desired.

*This is so hard! But I need to know what's on the other side of this trauma. I need to heal from past experiences.*

*Self-care is not selfish.*

With the help of a few simple steps and practices, I learned to love, accept and celebrate myself again. I'm no longer defined by a role or title but by the joy and fulfillment I bring into my life. I feel more confident and empowered than ever before, and it's translated into increased sexual pleasure. I have become a better mother, friend, and partner by focusing on myself. I know now that caring for myself is not selfish but an essential part of my well-being.

I am responsible for my happiness and joy.

# THE TOOL

Being busy with work, family, and social obligations can leave us drained and disconnected from our desires and needs. Prioritizing ourselves and pursuing passions is crucial for a fulfilling life, both in and out of the bedroom.

When we prioritize our pleasure and desires, we feel more confident and self-assured, become more magnetic to others, and connect with them on a deeper level. By cultivating a sense of passion, pleasure, and purpose, we bring vitality and excitement to our relationships.

Sex and intimacy are essential aspects of any healthy relationship. Focusing on our pleasure can help us connect with ourselves and our partners. When we know what we want and feel confident in expressing ourselves, we can create a more satisfying sexual experience during self-pleasure and time with our partners.

Putting ourselves first doesn't mean neglecting the needs of others. Instead, it means balancing caring for ourselves and nurturing our connections with those we love. When we feel fulfilled and energized, we can better show up for others and give generously from a place of abundance. As a female entrepreneur, the benefit of putting ourselves first and focusing on our well-being is increased productivity, creativity, and better client relationships.

## THE FOCUS ON YOU FORMULA

I created the *Focus On You* formula because, as busy women, we're natural nurturers. It's easy for us to focus more on our families while placing ourselves at the bottom of our daily priority list. Some days we might not be on our priority list at all. I created the formula from my own life experience. I can say that I used to feel busy and overwhelmed with family and household responsibilities and life in general. But now I know the benefit and importance of self-care, prioritizing my needs, and allowing myself to enjoy more passion, pleasure, and intimacy.

As a sex, intimacy, and body confidence coach, I understand how easy it is to lose sight of what is vital in our personal lives. Whether juggling work, family, and social obligations or simply trying to make it through each day without feeling overwhelmed with life, it's essential to remember that your sexuality and overall well-being matter. Now is a great time to focus on your passions, pleasures, and desires. Here are five tips, starting with the letters of the word FOCUS, to help you prioritize and enhance your life:

1. **F** - Free your mind
2. **O** - Open up to your desires
3. **C** - Connect with your body
4. **U** - Unlearn shame and guilt
5. **S** - Self-Care

## F - FREE YOUR MIND

The first step in this process is to free your mind for self-reflection. It's easy to lose your sense of self in the daily hustle and bustle of life and forget to take a moment to reflect on what you truly want and need. Create time for yourself each day—even just a few minutes. Use this time to do something that brings you joy. Examples are meditation, reading a book, taking a walk, or taking a nap. Any activity you enjoy that allows you to create space for quiet time to free your mind is a great place to start.

Regarding intimacy and pleasure, try setting aside some time each week to journal about your desires, fears, and goals related to your sexuality and overall well-being. Self-reflection can help you gain clarity, identify patterns, and make better choices. Begin small, with five to ten minutes weekly added to your schedule to get quiet and reflect. Gradually move to two to five minutes per day. As you slowly get used to making time for self-reflection (without guilt), you can enjoy five to ten minutes (or more) per day to focus on your desires and goals.

## O - OPEN UP TO YOUR DESIRES

Understanding and opening up to your desires is crucial for cultivating a fulfilling and satisfying life and sex life, regardless of age. We have a lifetime of experiences and beliefs that have shaped our life, sexuality, and desires. However, as we age, our bodies and desires can change, and it's essential to tune in and listen to what our bodies tell us. When we understand and acknowledge our desires, we can communicate them effectively and create deeper connections in our intimate relationships.

It's also essential to open up to your partner/partners. If you're in a relationship, it's vital to communicate openly and honestly with your partner about your desires and boundaries. Your partner is not a mind-reader, so don't be afraid to start a conversation about what you want to explore sexually, what you're uncomfortable with, and any concerns or insecurities you may have. Open communication can help build trust and deepen intimacy in your relationships. Your partner will likely appreciate your openness and willingness to explore.

## C - CONNECT WITH YOUR BODY

Connecting with your body on a deeper level is essential to unlock your passion, pleasure, and desires. When disconnected from our bodies, we don't fully experience all life offers. We become numb to the world and miss the joy of living. Our bodies are unique, complex, and beautiful! Take some time to explore and appreciate your body. Daily prayer and meditation are great ways to turn your focus within and connect with your power source.

Also, try new types of movement or exercise that feel good to you. Experiment with different kinds of touch or pleasure, and pay attention to how your body responds to the sensations. If you are new to exploring touch or uncomfortable with it, begin with gently caressing your skin and notice the sensations on your arm, leg, or hand. Notice the feelings at the point of contact and within other areas of your body. Connecting with your body can help increase confidence, pleasure, and overall well-being.

## U - UNLEARN SHAME AND GUILT

Many of us are conditioned to feel shame and guilt around our sexuality and desires. It's essential to recognize that these feelings are often based on outdated and harmful beliefs from religion, family, friends, or the societal narrative on sex and intimacy.

We are often told that we're not good enough, should be doing more, or are failing somehow. When it comes to our desires and pleasures, we might feel ashamed or guilty for even wanting them. Shame and guilt keep us from unlocking our genuine passion and joy. It is time to unlearn these harmful beliefs and prioritize our needs and desires. This is a challenging step. It requires us to confront our deepest fears and vulnerabilities. But it's a necessary part of the journey. By letting go of shame and guilt, we create space for joy and pleasure to enter our lives and permit ourselves to be fully alive and present.

## S - SELF-CARE

Finally, make sure to prioritize self-care in your life. Make time to enjoy activities and experiences that make you feel good. This looks different for everyone. Some ideas include making time for rest, engaging in activities that bring you joy, setting boundaries with work and social obligations, and seeking professional support when needed. Self-care is essential for overall well-being and can help you feel more confident, empowered, and fulfilled.

Practice self-care regularly. This might include getting enough sleep, eating well, exercising, and engaging in activities that help you relax and unwind. Set aside some time to get clear on your desires and goals. What brings you pleasure and fulfillment? What do you want to achieve in your life? Please write down your goals and take steps daily to move closer to them.

By focusing on self-reflection, desires, open communication, body connection, unlearning shame and guilt, and incorporating self-care practices into your daily routine, you can enhance your personal life and prioritize your sexuality with joy and pleasure. Prioritizing pleasure and sexuality as a female spiritual entrepreneur can lead to a more profound connection with oneself and one's spiritual path, leading to greater success in business and personal fulfillment.

You deserve to feel confident and fulfilled in all areas of your life.

Remember, putting yourself first isn't selfish—it's essential for creating a fulfilling and satisfying life. By focusing on your passions and desires, you can cultivate a sense of confidence and vitality that will enhance all aspects of your life, including love, pleasure, sex, and intimacy. So go ahead—indulge in your pleasure and watch as your relationships and life blossom.

## YOUR TURN

You've seen and done so many things,

your life has been filled with a range of feelings.

But now it's time to turn your focus inward,

to the passions that fuel your days moving forward.

For far too long, you've put others first,

their needs, their wants, and random outbursts.

But now it's time to focus on you

and everything you want to pursue.

Your passion is what fuels your fire.

Your pleasure is what you desire.

So take the time to nurture these,

and feel your spirit soar with ease.

Don't let the world dictate your path

or hold you back with doubt and wrath.

Embrace your dreams, your wants, and needs,

and watch as your soul feels all the feels.

For women, we know when it's time to shine,

put ourselves first, and embrace the feminine divine.

So, let's live life on our pleasurable terms

and feel the fire within that so brightly burns.

**Tamara Robinson** is a Sex & Intimacy Coach dedicated to helping individuals and couples find love and achieve fulfilling and satisfying sex lives. She has helped countless people boost self-confidence, overcome sexual challenges, explore desires, and enhance intimate connections.

As a divorced single mother, Tamara understands the challenges of balancing her personal and professional life and knows how to create a safe and nurturing environment for her clients. She is empathetic, non-judgmental, and committed to creating a safe space where people feel comfortable expressing intimate details of their desires and concerns.

When she is not coaching, Tamara enjoys relaxing bubble baths, dancing, writing, and meditation. These activities helped her cultivate a deep self-awareness and self-love, which she brings to her coaching practice. In her spare time, she studies female orgasms, sexual anatomy, and self-care techniques to enhance her knowledge and skills.

Tamara's journey of becoming a sex, intimacy & body confidence coach began at the age of 40 when she experienced a sexual awakening. This experience led her to embrace her femininity, explore her sexuality, and prioritize self-care in her daily routine. She understands firsthand the transformative power of sexual exploration and the importance of feeling confident and comfortable in one's body.

With Tamara as your coach, you can expect a compassionate, non-judgmental, and empowering experience. She is committed to helping you achieve your desires and personal goals and guiding you toward a more fulfilling and satisfying love life. Whether you're looking to find love, improve communication with your partner, explore your sexuality, or boost your body confidence, Tamara is here to support you on your journey.

Connect with Tamara to begin your path of reconnecting to your passion, pleasures, and desires: www.passionpleasurecoach.com

Instagram & Tiktok: @passionpleasurecoach

CHAPTER 6

# ESCAPE THE FEAR AND DO IT AFRAID

## DEVELOP DISCERNMENT, FIND YOUR PURPOSE, AND CHANGE STRESS INTO JOY

LaTisha Boyd-Potts, MSW, AMHFA, YMHFA

## MY STORY

The name of this chapter is very personal to me. To utter these very words: Escape; Fear; Discernment; Purpose; Stress; and Joy, I can see the breath leave my mouth, floating in the air like a cloud of smoke. I take a deep breath and say them slowly, one at a time, with relief that I've learned to trust myself wholeheartedly. The self-trust lesson did not come easy for me, but each decision was good and bad. I know the voice in me that guides me and has raised me from a little girl into this adult was a spiritual connection to my Higher Power with many faces and different names.

In my youth and young adult years, wounded by abuse and violence, fear was the driving force of my relationships with everyone and everything around me. I was dragged around by this heavy force; it felt like rocks taped to my shoulders. And because I carried these rocks around so well, only I knew they were there. I was a fearless little girl—the fighter when my cousin needed backup and the mouthpiece who would stand up for the underdog. But inside, I was shy, scared, and always felt unseen. I didn't start to enjoy life until age 46. That's when I escaped that fear, and the rocks came tumbling down.

At age 46, I experienced the most painful headaches. I already suffered from migraines, so headaches were a part of my normal life. I walked around for months taking medication and going to the doctor for check-ups and refills, telling myself: *I just need to reduce my stress, and the pain will subside so I can function.*

But my body was not built for this kind of pain; it was beyond a migraine, and I could not function. Not only did sunlight hurt, but every lighted room I entered was painful, creating double vision in my left eye. People's voices echoed and sounded so loud. To escape the pain, I called out sick from work and stayed in the house in the dark for any relief I could get.

After not getting a full night's sleep for days, on August 10, 2017, I sat on the edge of the bed with my feet dangling. I was scared to touch the floor for fear that the very touch of my feet planted would send excruciating pain from the bottom of my feet through the veins in my legs straight to my head. After a few minutes or so, this calm voice came to me as I sat there with my feet dangling and my eyes closed:

*Latisha, I want you to listen; I don't want you to be afraid anymore; this pain you're feeling is not normal. Lay back in bed. Soon as the sun comes up, you are going to call the doctor's office. In all the pain you are feeling, you will be as sweet as pie to the receptionist who will answer the phone. And you will ask him if you can see your doctor this morning. You will tell him your pain is beyond a ten and you would like to come in this morning—not for another medication refill, but to have an exam to see what is going on in your body. These headaches are not normal.*

I listened to the voice with no fear. I waited until 9:00 am to call my doctor's office, and without hesitation, I said the words and acted as sweet as pie, just as the voice instructed. In the 11 years I've been going to this doctor's office, the receptionist was always a woman. This morning the person who took my call was a man, just as the voice said.

**Ask him** *if you can see your doctor this morning.*

Trying to say what I was instructed, he heard my pain behind the sweet-as-pie, interjected and said, "She has a cancellation. Do you think you can get here by 10:30?" The only words my tongue could form to say were, "Thanks."

## A NEW JOURNEY BEGINS

That morning after seeing my doctor, she put me on a different medication that eased the pain fast and made it more tolerable to function. She referred me to a neurologist who referred me for an MRI. They couldn't schedule the MRI until August 23. At this point, I was afraid of what it could be, but until then, I did what I had been doing- taking medication and trying to reduce my stress.

On August 23, 2017, I was still afraid, yet functioning and doing as the voice instructed—to live. I went and got my MRI at 10:00 am and went to work after. Not less than two hours later, sitting in my cubicle, I got the call. In his flat, cold tone, the voice on the other end said, "You have a benign brain tumor; I need you to call this doctor today."

He sounded like a Department of Motor Vehicles employee from the 1980s whose main function was to give you the information after waiting in long lines for hours just to hear, "You have the wrong paperwork; next." He gave me the doctor's information and said, "He is the best at what he does." In shock that I was hearing this on the phone, the first thought that came to my mind was to ask him if I would die. My second thought was filled with anger: *Why did he tell me this over the phone?* When my lips moved, all I said was, "Okay, thank you."

I wished God had chosen a different messenger. Although his delivery of the news did not come with a cushion through the phone, he was right about the doctor.

After three months of going to radiation treatment with the best medical team led by the doctor who created the Radio Surgery procedure for my medical condition, my whole mindset shifted.

One evening as I was writing in my journal, that voice spoke to me again. It was that voice that lives in between hope and abilities, that healthy spot in our minds that plays the reels of the good things in our lives. As I started to write my self-reflection, my fingers couldn't move, but my mouth opened. I lifted my hands high and began singing praises to God: *Thank you God for helping me to the end of the road.*

I visualized myself traveling and speaking at a conference, writing books that inspire others, and walking on the beach in Hawaii with a big straw hat on my head, sipping a pina colada, and taking in all the sunlight I could stand. At that moment, I learned the spirit of discernment, to listen without control, and to trust my Higher Power no matter what the outcome. My motivation engine was at full blast, and hope guided me in for a smooth landing. I looked forward to finding a greater purpose.

With my mind set on a journey of my choosing, a master's degree in social work, and twenty years of being on the front line, I now realize I've been growing in my purpose for several years: Helping others cope with mental health diagnoses and to function in their community and live quality lives. This is a job that requires tough skin and youthful motivation. I know the abilities I have to engage with and encourage others, especially when people are at their most vulnerable, aren't just a part of social science but a spiritual gift.

I choose to keep moving forward in joy and look toward purposeful life experiences. Why would God have created this beautiful earth with so many people and not lead us toward a purpose in helping each other? He has given all humans different gifts and talents.

In the isolation of 2020, my ideas continued to grow. I listen for the positive in the negative news reports and conversations. Anything I hear about anxiety, fear, death, or trauma becomes a workshop to heal and empower, a group chat to prevent, or a safe place where positive energy flows.

After many journeys and several roadblocks to becoming this empowered woman, God's timing could not be any more exact than now. He aligned every good spirit and light to shine on me from birth to this very moment. And today, we live in a time when people don't have to carry the shame of having a mental health diagnosis or seek help in an emotional crisis. It's okay to share our feelings in a safe space without fear or judgment, where healing can come in the form of positive energy, believing in yourself, or declaring a healing mantra. I don't doubt that kindness and empathy with a good laugh can bring joy to a broken spirit faster than it takes aspirin to circulate through the entire nervous system.

That specific voice that came to me on August 10, 2017, was a spirit that lives in me and once again saved my life. We all have a guiding spirit in us. Mine has protected me my entire life by putting a band-aid on bad decisions and celebrating with me through the good ones, like proud parents on graduation day.

I call the voice that spoke to me that night *My Spirit Woman*. Despite my ego, I try my best to always listen. To remind myself that I'm not that shy little girl or an unseen person. *My Spirit Woman* allows me to be fearless even when faced with a situation that calls for me to be afraid, and I do it anyway. To keep this confidence, I developed this tool to define who I am by simply using the meaning and spelling of my name. This is one way I stay connected with inspired energy. This tool aids in building self-esteem and self-love. It can be done by anyone from youth to seniors. The goal is to inspire yourself every day, especially those hard days when doubt creeps in and the imposter syndrome shows up, like those days when you're chosen to pitch your business on a Zoom meeting or hanging out having fun with other women. I have created what is called a "Praise Phrase," which I use as a mantra to inspire myself. I've chosen to hang my mantra in the bathroom, where I'm sure to see it and say it every day. You can also record it on your favorite device and save it as a screen saver. This allows you to become your own positive force.

# THE TOOL

**Step 1 Origin:** Everything has an origin. Learn the meaning of your name, and if you don't like what you find, guess what? You can change what you want to be called. Remember, our names were chosen for us at birth—first, middle, and last. This builds confidence as an entrepreneur and a person. You'll introduce yourself to several people, and you want them to know you believe in yourself and the name of your business.

My name: LaTisha Rachel Boyd-Potts. My mother and my aunt named me.

According to Google, my name **Latisha** is a feminine name of Spanish origin. Coming from the Latin name Letitia, it means happiness, joy, or gladness.

Also, according to Google, an American variation of the Latin *Letitia*, Latisha is an "artful allure." A meeting of two eras, **Latisha** comes from the medieval name **Laetitia,** with the same meaning of joy or gladness. Over the centuries, the name continued to evolve though its sentiments never altered.

**Rachel** comes from Genesis chapter 29, the first book in the bible (Old Testament), a story I'm most fascinated with as it describes a woman who grew in her purpose and became an intercessor for the people of Israel, as God chose her life's journey. Really! Unbelievable, right!?

I hyphenate Boyd-Potts because Boyd was my mother's married name to her first husband, not my biological father's last name. She became a widow at 23 years old. Her husband's death benefits allowed her to provide for her three daughters. Becoming a single mother at 22 years old helped me understand and realize how smart that was of her. So, I honored her with the hyphenation, and my husband understood how important it was for me to keep the name.

Once you have your origin, you can always go back and reflect for inspiration and growth.

**Step 2 Compliments:** List three compliments about yourself:

1. ................................................................................................
2. ................................................................................................
3. ................................................................................................

**Step 3 Doing it Afraid:** Think about a task that made you nervous and that you still completed. Add more lines if needed.

................................................................................................

................................................................................................

................................................................................................

**Step 4: Your Praise Phrase:** Read aloud what you wrote in Step 3. This is particularly important and cannot be missed. At the end of the third time, state the following Praise Phrase: "Glory be! You did that (add your name)."

Next, say the Praise Phrase and attach a complimentary word or words from Step 2 at the end of your name. It should sound like this: "Glory be! You did that, LaTisha! You're a force of nature growing every day."

Now you have a mantra that came from within to encourage yourself.

Here is where the power is born. How do you know if it is working?

The first time you read aloud, the idea is to listen. The second time, the focus is to feel the emotion. And the third time, it's to affirm the positive spirit that is now involved. After the third time, if you're smiling and feel the emotion of that wow factor, it's working.

I'm sure you speak to yourself in a form of motivation that's similar, but I guarantee you don't do it often enough. You can also create your Praise Phrase.

After incorporating this tool, I changed the spelling of my name because now I had big shoes to fill—mine! Today my name and signature appear as " LaTisha." For me, that capital T is saying, "I am courageous! I am seen! I am Spirit Woman!" It makes me feel good when I sign my name.

You now have a little history of the name Rachel and why I accepted the name Boyd after surviving divorce and declaring I'd never be loved or married ever again. Unexpectedly, in the positive energy of enjoying my life, I changed; my inner light was no longer dull. My attitude was happy, and my spirit of joy was contagious. Two years later, I met my husband, who shared the same values of love and marriage. And that confirms my last name—Potts.

**LaTisha Boyd-Potts,** MSW, AMHFA, YMHFA, Founder and Owner of Grouplady Lifeskills Consulting, LLC, is a natural motivational speaker and community life coach with a master's degree in social work. She is certified in adult and youth mental health first aid, specializing in an integrated approach to psycho-education that provides a safe space for people to learn about mental health diagnoses and build emotional wellness from conference rooms to classrooms. She has 20 years of expertise in direct social work practice, group work, and crisis intervention. She has a deep appreciation of the social work profession and an understanding of humans as social beings.

LaTisha is Spirit Woman, the daughter of the late Carolyn Boyd-Acker and the youngest of two sisters. She is a devoted wife and mother of two adult sons, two grandkids, and three fur babies. She's fulfilled in finding peace in things around her, loves theater art, and enjoys a good therapy session once in a while (retail therapy).

Connect with LaTisha:

Website:
https://www.Groupladylifeskills.com
https://www.Alignable.com

Facebook: https://www.Facebook.com/GLC

Instagram: https://www.instagram.com/grouplady.llc/

Email: lbp.grouplady@gmail.com

CHAPTER 7

# JOURNEY TO WHOLENESS

## THE PATH TO SELF-ACCEPTANCE AND CREATING THE BUSINESS YOU LOVE

Jacqueline (Jackie) R. Scott, JD, ML

*"Because one believes in oneself, one doesn't try to convince others. Because one is content with oneself, one doesn't need others' approval. Because one accepts oneself, the whole world accepts him or her."*

~ Lao Tzu

I was 11 years old when money first hurt me. I learned money hurts, disappoints, limits, and controls your life.

## INTRODUCTION

Have you ever felt like you're not good enough, not worthy enough, or not deserving enough of the things you want in life? Have you ever struggled with self-doubt, self-criticism, or self-judgment that held you back from pursuing your entrepreneurial dreams and passions?

I have. For years it kept me stuck. I'd helped countless others build their dreams, yet I remained unfulfilled and unable to build my own. It wasn't until after years of "doing my work" that I realized the key to my ability to step fully into doing what I love was to first love and accept myself. I had to be willing to embrace all aspects of myself, both positive and negative, without judgment or conditions. Be willing to ask myself tough questions, identify and challenge the stories of my past, and equally embrace the gifted and flawed parts of my being that are authentically me. This was the core of my journey toward wholeness.

Achieving wholeness and self-acceptance can, in turn, help you create the business you love by enhancing your confidence, creativity, resilience, and authenticity. If you understand *you*, then you are easily able to identify your *"why,"* which is key to sustaining your momentum during challenging times. My goal is to inspire you to embark on your own journey to wholeness and self-acceptance and to discover the benefits it can bring to your life and work.

# MY STORY

I tucked that narrative about money deep inside my 11-year-old self and held on to it for decades.

I remember it like yesterday. It was a good day. School was so much fun. The warmth of the sun beamed down on Wendy and me as we raced off the school bus and skip-raced down the street—our usual pastime.

"I'll meet you in the front soon as I change my clothes and grab my snack," I said. Mom would kill me if I messed up my school clothes.

"Don't forget your bat!" I continued. I couldn't wait to try out my new glove. I was really proud of it. I saved up my allowance and was able to pay for half all by myself. Mom paid for the other half. She kept her promise. I beamed on the way home from the store, already planning on what to save up for next.

"Who's that in your yard?" Wendy asked, "Your mom home?"

As we got closer, my stomach turned. The hair on the back of my neck tickled. My skips turned to steps. My feet became heavier and heavier. I struggled to focus; with each step, things went from foggy to clear and clear to foggy.

*Why is the couch outside? My bed, my books, mom's clothes. Is that her favorite coat? Why are our clothes in a pile in the driveway?*

Feeling nauseous, I couldn't breathe. Panic set in.

"Boots! Boots!" I screamed, "Where's Boots?!" I felt the tears welling up, overflowing hot onto my cheeks. My heart raced. "Where's my cat?!" My voice fluctuated between a demand and a plea.

The men never even looked at me, never acknowledged me. They just kept tossing our stuff out into the driveway.

I was eleven.

"Mom! Mom!" I yelled and cried. I needed my mom.

I knew inside that yelling was useless. She was on her way home from school, probably picking up my baby brother right about now. There were no cell phones back then.

Tears flowed heavier now, my cheeks burning from the hot sun and the warmth of the flood coming from my eyes. I couldn't breathe. There was nothing to do but wait. At that moment, through my tears, I spotted it in the dirt, my new glove. I'd forgotten Wendy was there beside me watching all of this. She must have seen it, too, because she ran over and grabbed it off the ground before I could say anything. Blurred in the distance, through my tears, I saw her dusting it off, running back towards me. No words, just eye-to-eye; my best friend handed me the glove, tags still on.

"I'll go get my mom," she whispered, "She'll know what to do."

I shook my head, turned, and made my way over to my favorite tree in the yard. Sliding down, my back against its hearty trunk to stabilize me, I slumped to the ground. It was then that I spotted her under the porch. "Boots! Boots! Come 'er girl!" I called. Shivering in fear, she ran into my lap, and there we sat together and waited. The men never even looked at me, never acknowledged me.

I will never forget the look in her eyes. Tired from a long day of teaching, this was supposed to be an evening off. One of the rare times she didn't have to go to her evening job. These were the days I got extra time after dinner to play outside, as long as my homework was done, of course. Wendy and I looked forward to these days. Today was different. Pulling up frantically, sheer panic all over her face, grabbing my brother from the back seat, Mom raced over to make sure I was okay.

"Are you hurt?" she asked. Relieved that she was there but not okay, I could only shake my head no. "It will be okay." She did her best to reassure me. "Stay here with your brother."  Minutes turned into what felt like hours. All I can remember hearing was the word *money*.

"Miss, do you have the *money?*"

"Sorry, without the *money,* we have no choice."

"Please, I just need a few more days to get the *money.*"

"Okay, okay, can you just give me a few minutes to call my parents to see if they can get the *money?*"

She walked heavily back over to our tree. "Don't worry honey; it's just *money;* we will be okay. She reached over and cradled both of us. We have each other. God loves us. He will take care of us. Mommy loves you." We sat rocking, the three of us, in unison.

They never gave her the chance to get the *money.*

On my journey to wholeness, what I learned about myself was my perception of money kept me bound in a complex set of emotions ranging from joy to fear. My head and skill told me it was necessary; no business can function without money. Yet my heart resisted being bound by it because I associated it with pain. My response to my emotions was to minimize money. I convinced myself: *It's not about the money; it's about my calling to serve.* In truth, I acted out of the fear that money might once again disappoint me.

Once I identified and accepted this about myself, I could look at all the ways it impacted and stunted my entrepreneurial spirit. Facing my brokenness and vulnerability freed me from the shame and bondage money held over my life and my ability to excel. Once freed, I was able to move from bound to bountiful.

What stories are you telling yourself that are keeping you bound?

# THE TOOL

## THE PETALS OF SELF-DISCOVERY

Entrepreneurship is an exciting journey requiring courage, determination, and faith. It's not just about starting a business or making money. After all, do you just want a job, or do you want a mission? Are you creating work or living into a vocation, a calling? This is about pursuing a vision, creating (adding) value, and making a positive impact on those you serve. Whether just starting out or a veteran, you know this journey takes stamina. It involves stepping outside your comfort zone, taking calculated risks, and having faith in yourself and your abilities even when others don't. Embracing the uncertainty of entrepreneurship and having the confidence to pursue your dreams starts with you.

Entrepreneurship calls on you to tap into your whole self. It's my hope the five steps below will provide you with a path to self-discovery and acceptance to help you build and sustain the business you love. There are no right or wrong answers. In fact, as you work the steps, you might find that each discovery leads to another layer of questions. That's the beauty of self-discovery, it's a journey. Grab a pen and jump in!

**Step 1: Becoming:** Answering the question *How I Became Me:*

- Let's start from the beginning. To launch your exploration into wholeness, let's look at your connections from birth. In this step, we explore two levels:
    - Your Parents: Who are/were they? Where were they from? What was their relationship like? What was your relationship with them?
    - Your Birth: Where were you born? What were the circumstances of your birth? (Explore things like: were your parents married? Were you healthy at birth? etc.)

These connections are the earliest lessons we learn about relationships, bonding, and trust. What adjectives come to mind when you think about these lessons?

***Business Tip:*** *Being a self-aware entrepreneur who understands your emotions and behaviors is important to success. According to Entrepreneur Magazine, self-awareness helps you determine if entrepreneurship is right for you, helps you leverage your strengths, and develop an authentic brand.*

**Step 2: My Tribe:** Exploring *Who Influences Me:*

- First, examine your familial relationships: Who are your siblings? Where do you fall within them? How would you describe your relationship? If no siblings, take a moment to explore what it felt like as an only child. How good were you at building relationships?
- Next, let's examine friends and other non-familial relationships: Who are/were your best friends growing up and now? Who are the people who were like family to you? How do you describe those relationships?

Think about what emerged in Step 1 for you about relationships and bonding. What effect did those lessons have on the relationships you note here in Step 2?

***Business Tip:*** *Business is relational. Building and maintaining relationships is very important to being a successful entrepreneur. According to Forbes, building relationships helps you gain more clients, increases positive client experience, and can increase your professional footprint.*

**Step 3: My Joys:** What are the Celebratory Moments in my life:

- Let's explore the following:
    - What brings you joy?
    - What brought/brings your family joy?
    - What were those joyful moments you shared with your family?
    - What were/are your most memorable celebrations and achievements? Were they your achievements or others?

As you list your answers, think about things like who you celebrated with. Were there any other emotions associated with your celebrations? (ex. Sometimes people experience guilt when something good happens). Explore how you processed joy and celebrations growing up and how you process them now as an adult.

***Business Tip:*** *According to Forbes, happiness plays a significant role in an entrepreneur's journey. It contributes to your ability to develop a clear vision and purpose and helps when you must overcome challenges and failures when they come your way.*

**Step 4: My Pain:** When did I experience pain or challenges:

- Here we will explore the following:
    - What were the challenges, losses, disappointments, and/or traumas you experienced?
    - At what ages did they occur?
    - How were they handled?
    - Did people (family, friends, etc.) talk about them?
    - Did they process them with you?
    - What were your feelings?

Like with the questions you processed with celebrations, and to the extent you can, explore whether you experienced any other emotions associated with the traumatic or challenging circumstances identified, i.e., anger, fear, depression, etc. Take your time here, step back, breathe into this, stop if you need to, and move forward when you're ready.

***Business Tip:*** *Being a resilient entrepreneur will help you adapt and improve in quickly changing environments and maintain motivation, optimism, and perseverance in critical situations.*

**Step 5: ME:** Examining Why I am. . .:

This is the step where we look closely at the full equation and add up the answers from steps 1 through 4. Where has the path led us? Here is where we examine our core by asking the following:

- What are my values?
- Where did they come from?
- What is my relationship to/with faith and spirituality?
- How do my gender, race, culture, and geographical connection impact or influence how I define myself?

This is where the lightbulb went off for me on my journey to wholeness. I had to accept that my emotional push-pull relationship with money was self-limiting and causing me to engage in self-sacrificing behaviors. One can't possibly build a business and fear money or not want to deal with it. Yet I'd found a way to hide from it in plain sight by helping everyone else build and lead their ventures so I didn't have to. I stayed constantly on the move, running in fear that it (money) would once again hurt and disappoint me. It wasn't until I sat with myself and came face to face with the trauma I experienced as a child and the resulting emotions of fear, grief, pain, and disappointment that I could heal, accept, and fully embrace my value.

**Business Tip:** *According to Entrepreneur Magazine, knowing your WHY is one of, if not the most important parts of your entrepreneurship journey. Your mission, your purpose, and your passion are the driving forces of your business. Your WHY keeps you on track and motivated to excel.*

Where are you on your Journey to Wholeness? Once you complete the Five Steps, ask yourself:

- What new or additional questions are coming up for me?
- What were my aha moments? What did I learn about myself as I examined each step?
- How can I respond to my aha moments?
- On a scale of 1-10, how ready am I to accept and embrace me?
- What do I need to move forward towards full self-acceptance and to excel?

Welcome to the Journey. There are wonderful things for you to discover. Jump in and *Embrace YOU!*

**Jackie Scott,** JD, ML, is a wife and mother of three who is passionate about lifting and supporting women. She is an author, national speaker, and trainer who leverages her executive leadership experience and skills to tap into the strengths of her clients and build their capacity to excel. Trained in both Law and Business, Jackie is a seasoned executive known for strong people and strategic skills. With over 25 years of multi-sector experience, including government, private and non-profit sectors, she provides her clients with practical insights and strategies to help them rise above and beyond to achieve their goals.

With her faith and family at the center of all she does, Jackie finds joy in spending time with her crew. Whether gathered as a family watching their favorite sports teams; binging the newest series or movie; or just enjoying a good laugh over a silly joke, she believes it's these simple moments in life that provide her with the most clarity of purpose.

Jackie has been featured in the book How to Be an Emotionally Intelligent Leader, By Cheryl O'Donoghue; and is a featured collaborative author in Reinvented to Rise II, by Visionary Author Dr. Alethia Tucker.

Jackie holds a dual BA from Georgetown University, a Juris Doctor from the Georgetown University Law Center, and a Masters in Leadership from the McDonough School of Business at Georgetown. She also studied Pastoral Counseling at Loyola University in Maryland.

As a mentor-coach, Jackie's mission is to walk alongside women and support them as they embrace their true selves, leverage their strengths, and harness their power.

She is guided daily by her life scripture Isaiah 50: 4-7 (NIV).

Connect with Jackie on the following:

LinkedIn: https://www.linkedin.com/in/jacqueline-scott-jd-ml-4378ba/

Instagram: https://www.instagram.com/jackiebscott93/

Email: expressurself247@gmail.com

CHAPTER 8

# CLARIFY WHAT YOU WANT

## THE FIRST STEP TO FINDING YOUR PURPOSE AND REACHING YOUR GOALS

Maria Petrucci, D.C.

## MY STORY

It was my first or second year of college when I heard the priest say, "Why do we go to church every Sunday? It's important to not only follow church rules but to know why we have them."

*Wow, what?! What do you mean 'Why do we go to church every Sunday'? Aren't we supposed to; do we have a choice? I'll have to think about this.*

I couldn't come up with a good reason why I had to go to church, so I stopped. I also stopped my "fear of God" and of going to Hell, which were so prominent in my young life.

*Is everything I was previously told or taught up for discussion? Who am I, apart from what other people told me how to be all my life? What about all those other rules I was taught to follow?*

This began my quest for answers about life and who I was.

About two years later, I was on a path to a different spiritual understanding of the world and my place in it. "I read this book, and I'm recommending that you all read it too," was my older brother's advice to me and my sisters and brothers the summer before my senior year of college. "It's called *Yoga, Youth, and Reincarnation."* With an open mind and feeling a powerful resonance, I voraciously read that book and did the yoga positions it described. It was like I had come home. It resonated so strongly. There were ideas and ways of living I knew nothing about, but they all sounded so right.

After graduating college with a B.A. in psychology, I went exploring to discover what I wanted to do with the rest of my life. I was contemplating more schooling. *Psych counseling? Nutrition?* Both were vying for first place. *Maybe some sort of natural healing profession?* I was taking a class in nutrition when my dad said, "You should go see my chiropractor; it sounds like something you'd like." The chiropractor encouraged me to follow him in his chosen profession. "You can use nutrition in your office along with chiropractic care." So, I researched and weighed my options and finally decided to go to chiropractic school.

A couple of years later, I was on a plane to the Los Angeles College of Chiropractic to learn the basics for my new career choice and experience the unique and cool things about the L.A. area I read so much about. California was the birthplace of so many new ideas and beautiful landscapes. I made new friends and acquired a wealth of knowledge both in and outside of school. One of those places was the Religious Science community, which greatly added to my philosophy of life.

*Mental cause of physical disease and ailments? Using your thoughts to make something happen in your life?* I was intrigued. The seeds had probably already been planted with the yoga book about ten years earlier, as well as with other books I had read since then. I even took the "A Course in Miracles" class, staying in California for another year before moving back to Maryland.

Ready to start my new life as a chiropractor, I returned home, where my dad helped me set up shop and sent me new patients. It wasn't long before, through a series of new connections, I felt led to attend a four-year course in Spiritual Science in Baltimore.

"Pay attention to your thoughts" was one of the ideas in a book we read the first year. *Here it is again. What about the mental/emotional cause of physical conditions? If physical pain can come from emotional or mental blocks, how do I incorporate this into my practice?*

I ran into this idea in various ways, including through Candace Pert's book, *Molecules of Emotion*. It scientifically supported the idea that emotions and beliefs can lodge in our bodies and cause physical as well as mental/emotional ailments. I noticed a few patients who experienced emotional releases during my work with them. I talked with massage therapists and other body workers who experienced the same.

In my search, I tried different ways of getting to the emotional/mental cause of my patients' pain and discomfort, but I kept running into blocks.

*I really want to get this right; I think it would make it easier for me to help people heal more deeply. Help them find work they like, enjoy their lives and have it not be so hectic. But it's not working; I must be doing it wrong,* I told myself after trying yet another new technique or test. It took me some time before I finally realized these weren't the right fit for ME, not that I was doing it "wrong."

*Feel into what's right for you, Maria. Don't try to make it work. Try something else.*

Over the years, since my work wasn't going the way I wanted on many levels, I sought out a business coach or two. After approaching one, she told me, "You need to start with personal coaching before you get any business coaching."

One of the first things my coach had me do was read her book, starting with suggestions for physical self-care and establishing healthy habits. I flew through this section, checking off all the boxes and congratulating myself for doing so well in this area already. When I got to the section that included emotions, self-talk, and interactions with other people, I realized I could use a lot more personal growth and healing.

My attempts at personal growth in previous years mostly involved reading self-help books. I wasn't very good at applying what I learned, embodying it, so to speak, at least for the difficult parts of my life and in my work. I was feeling stuck and blocked.

*My business is not going well. I don't know how to promote myself. I have to do everything myself. I feel like I'm stagnating; I have no power to change things.*

Something occurred to me. I thought I had dropped my fear of being judged by God and going to Hell a long time ago, but now I realized all that earlier fear had landed in my head and heart as self-criticism, self-doubt, and low self-esteem. I was trying to be perfect. I didn't express myself or my feelings well. I was very shy and afraid to speak up. I was afraid of what others might think. I let fear prevent me from moving forward. Soon I noticed, yes, I no longer feared God or his judgment, but now I was judging myself and what I was doing (or not doing)!

Once I started getting help from various coaches and challenging myself to do the things I was afraid of, especially speaking in front of a group, I started to feel different. I felt more empowered and capable of transformation, even if it meant taking small steps. I learned that the "bad" things that show up in life work *for* us, directing us to learn a new skill or overcome a fear rather than blocking us from achieving what we want. The thing is not to ignore them or try to push them away but to look at them and see what they are telling us. Feel what's going on inside, ask for help from others, including a Higher (kinder) Power, and take time out for reflection and journaling.

I started making changes in the last several years and uncovered many blocks. I started speaking up more and being more comfortable giving presentations. I began paying attention to my mindset and becoming more aware of and accepting of my emotions.

I started thinking even before the pandemic, *I need to find a way to work remotely that helps people heal more deeply. Maybe I can learn distance healing. Maybe I can offer a course. Maybe I can teach through writing.* Then the covid pandemic hit, and I decided *no more putting this off; now's the time.* I learned long-distance healing using CranioSacral Therapy as a starting point. I practiced using PowerPoint to focus my thoughts and do presentations online. I used affirmations to get in touch with my self-talk and how I was feeling.

I worked through enough of my blocks to offer a six-week course on elevating your own healing power. This would be my way of offering tools for getting to the mental/emotional cause of pain and stress as well as for reaching goals.

# THE TOOL

When I began to turn my life around more consciously, I noticed a consistent phenomenon when I took steps toward a new goal, especially when it was particularly important or challenging.

The image that came to my mind was a circle. It went from an idea to planning or acting on the idea to getting stuck to moving through blocks to taking inspired action to finally reaching my goal and then going upward to the next level or goal. The process I developed to help move through these steps more easily has about five main components, the first of which is "clarify."

There are many ways to get clear on your big purpose or mission, as well as the many smaller meaningful decisions that go into having a business that aligns with who you are. Listening to what's going on deep inside you and following where you're led is key. Maybe something someone says resonates with you and sends you in a different direction. Maybe you go on vacation or a retreat and your soul speaks to you. The tool I'm sharing can be used in your day-to-day life. It's an expansion of the way I was originally taught to use affirmations.

The benefits of getting clear before starting on your journey include:

- Greater recognition or focus on your values.
- Knowing whether your goal is yours and not what someone else thinks it should be.
- Being more efficient with your time, money, and energy.

Here is my tool for clarifying what you want, why you want it, and how you want to feel when you've accomplished your goals. And, how to foster those feelings even before you reach them.

## CLARIFY

### PART 1 GETTING STARTED

1. Start with a general idea of a goal for improving or creating something new in your business. For example, maybe it's getting to know your customers/clients/patients better. Maybe it's about bringing in more

income with fewer expenses. Maybe it's a new service you'd like to introduce.

2. Part of clarifying is connecting, so take a few deep breaths, get rid of any distractions, and connect with what's going on inside your head and your body.

3. Take a piece of paper or use a Word document and write down everything that comes up around your goal or intention. Write in a stream-of-consciousness way, and don't worry about punctuation or accuracy. Include the "good" and the "bad," and everything in between that comes to mind. You may notice that what comes out depends on the mood you start with. For example, if you're frustrated, confused, or angry, you may release much of that in your writing. If you're in a happy place, you may get an energy boost or feel more confident and excited. When you start the process, you may know more about what you don't want rather than what you do want, but this will help you get started.

4. Take another piece of paper or use a new Word document and make two columns. Then summarize, in bullet form, all the negative and limiting beliefs, thoughts, images, feelings, and circumstances that came through in your writing and put them in the left-hand column labeled "What I Don't Want" or "Challenges." For example, these might include activities and responsibilities, self-talk, perspectives, and other people involved.

5. Label the right-hand column "What I Want" or "Solutions/Goal" and do the same as above around what you have now that you want to keep and what you don't have but want to include as part of your goal.

6. Go back to the list of things you don't want on the left. What does it tell you about what you *do* want? If it's something different from what you've already written on the right (what you want), think about what it's saying as far as what you *do* want and write it in the right-hand column. For instance, go from "I'm frustrated that I have to do everything myself" to "I get lots of help from people who like doing the things I don't."

## PART 2 CREATE AN AFFIRMATION

1. Look at your positive, right-hand entries and picture your goal already accomplished.

2. From these, write a few positive statements about your goal, how it feels, and what it looks like, using descriptive, uplifting words. Use "I" or "my" as part of your statements, e.g., "I see," "I am," "I have," "I feel," or "My life."

3. See if you can condense your description into one or two sentences or a brief phrase. If not, you can shorten it later; although, there are also advantages to keeping it long.

   **EXAMPLE:** "I love the people in my class, and they are all benefiting from the exercises I have developed."

4. Add at the end, "This or something better for the highest good of all concerned. And so, it is!" or something equivalent. This statement reminds you that there may be an even better way of experiencing/having what you want than you can imagine at this time.

## PART 3 USE YOUR AFFIRMATIONS TO FURTHER CLARIFY

1. Write your affirmation(s) out long-hand, type them on the computer, or say them out loud five to ten times a day. In the process, go inward and notice how you're feeling and any self-talk that arises. See below—Questions and Observations—for some tips on what to look for when you tune into yourself.

2. This process is flexible. You can change your goal or affirmation along the way as your vision shifts into more of what you want. You can also incorporate confidence-bolstering or self-appreciation words. For example, "I am great at _____ and enjoy it immensely." You may especially want to do this when you notice any limiting beliefs or thoughts that come up.

3. Use your affirmation for as long as it is helpful. If you want to replace limiting thoughts with more uplifting and empowering ones, you'll need to be consistent. It takes at least 21 days to stop your automatic thinking and change it to something new. If you want to cement it, continue for another round or two of 21 days (63 total).

4. Alternatively, when you feel you've gained positive momentum, you may want to stop for a while. You can pick it back up if you need it again for inspiration or greater clarification.

5. Remember, don't hold too tightly to your words. Make sure you feel better when you write or say them and let the Universe/God guide you to your next step.

## QUESTIONS AND OBSERVATIONS TO CONSIDER WHEN YOU WRITE YOUR AFFIRMATIONS:

1. Notice how you feel emotionally and physically. Does your body tighten up, or do you feel uplifted and lighter?

2. Does your statement/paragraph flow and feel right? Does it ring true for you?

3. Check to see if your goal is yours and doesn't come from what someone else thinks you should do.

4. Pay attention to your self-talk—are you having doubts about yourself? Do you feel inauthentic? Do you lack confidence or belief that you can accomplish your goal? Are you blaming others for it not happening? Or do you feel confident, sure, trusting, and excited?

You may want to journal more if you hit an emotional storm. This is when you're overwhelmed with a rush of difficult or conflicting feelings. Journal about any mental blocks or stories that come up. Get them out of your head and onto paper or a document as before. Consider keeping, in a separate place, a list of the objections/blocks/challenges that come up when you write your affirmations. They often repeat themselves. You may need to set some extra time aside to work through the especially difficult or repetitive limiting beliefs that arise. It's good that they're rising to the surface, and you're aware of them. It allows you to let go and transmute the blocks that hold you back so you can transform your life.

My wish is that this tool helps you rise to the occasion when the going gets rough and that you also use it before that happens. May your business be all you dreamed of and more!

**Maria Petrucci,** D.C. is a healer focusing on chiropractic care, craniosacral therapy, and mind-body tools. She helps people align, relax, and let go of pain or discomfort in their bodies and minds. She has practiced chiropractic for almost 40 years, using nutrition and energy-related healing methods and remedies with her chiropractic treatment so her patients can heal without drugs or surgery whenever possible. Maria blends her modalities for a more comprehensive healing experience. Her vision is to seamlessly incorporate emotional and mental release into her hands-on healing work for a truly holistic treatment and to help people live their purpose.

At home, Maria enjoys time with her humorous writer-and-retired-history-teacher husband, Jay Seaborg, and special, funny, Panera-working "spy-tective" daughter, Erin Seaborg. She loves meditation, yoga, jigsaw-puzzling, wordle-ing, walking in a nearby Mt. Airy, Maryland park, and keeping in touch with family.

You can find and connect with Maria on her website:
https://mariapetruccidc.com
or Facebook page:
https://www.facebook.com/MariaPetrucciDC

Learn the full outline of the Self-C.A.R.E. process on her website and email her if you'd like future announcements about classes and books.

# CHAPTER 9

# CHANGE TALK

## 5 KEYS TO MASTERING CHANGE

Gail Dixon

## MY STORY

Striding confidently to the podium, I prepared to do something I'd done hundreds of times before—deliver a speech. It should've been old hat, the easiest thing in the world. Instead, it was a disaster—one that changed my life and taught me how to master change rather than letting it master me.

I was a talker all my life, even when I wasn't supposed to be talking. I talked in church and school when silence was the rule. I talked to my sisters at bedtime, even after they fell asleep. And when there was nobody else to talk to, I talked to myself.

I loved words and the power they had to make things happen. I knew I would be making my living using words, I just didn't know how. I planned on being a teacher, imagining myself telling my students about the wonders of the world. It didn't quite turn out that way at first, but I think that's exactly where I've ended up.

Back to that minute at the podium. I was the presenter at a conference focusing on substance abuse prevention. My job was to convince the audience that spending at least as much on prevention as we did on treatment was a wise investment. Not a difficult task, at least in my mind.

Head up, shoulders back. Gazing over the heads of people in the room, I focused on a spot in the back; I prepared to aim my voice at the person standing against the far wall. Taking a breath, I opened my mouth to speak.

Nothing came out. Not one single word. I tried again. And a third time. Still nothing.

By this time, the audience was growing restless, and I was growing more and more breathless. Signaling for my boss, seated on the dais beside the podium, I wrote a note, "Can't breathe. Can't talk." I slid my notes to her and walked away from the podium and off the platform, barely stepping off the last step before hitting the ground.

Waking in the ambulance, I was dazed and confused and felt the weight of the oxygen mask on my face. I heard the voices of the paramedics but couldn't make out the words. Even with the oxygen, it felt as though I could not pull in enough air. My heart raced. *What on Earth is going on?* I wondered.

After more tests than I'd had in all my life combined, the verdict was to send me to another hospital for yet another round of tests and specialists. Meanwhile, I couldn't breathe without the oxygen.

"Paralyzed diaphragm" was the diagnosis. And then came the search for a cause so we could determine the cure. Meanwhile, my life was turned upside down in more ways than I could count. Everything I thought I knew about managing change was put to the test and didn't begin to make me feel better, mentally or physically.

All the platitudes like, "Just keep trying," "It will eventually be all right," "You'll get used to the new normal," and "Just pray and God will see you through" fell short. I couldn't do my job; I couldn't breathe without being tethered to an oxygen concentrator or portable tank. I lived in fear of a power failure, and time away from home was measured by how much oxygen remained in the portable tank.

My energy for the day was exhausted by the time I showered in the morning. Getting into the car was an ordeal, as was anything that put pressure on my diaphragm—bending to tie my shoes, trying to get into the bathtub, or getting into water above my waist in the swimming pool. I slept sitting up in a chair, with the footrest up, but unable to recline. I couldn't even hold a very long conversation without getting out of breath.

I felt disheartened, discouraged, and defeated. None of the doctors could determine a cause for the paralyzed diaphragm. Without a cause, they couldn't offer a prognosis, so I had no idea if my condition was as good as it would be or as bad as it would ever be. Should I hope for something better or hope for nothing worse?

Simply put, I was living a life that was totally unfamiliar to me. I didn't know who I was anymore. I thought I knew about handling change, but nothing prepared me for this loss of identity.

Finding my way around and through to the other side was a long and arduous process, one I navigated with help from every corner of my life. My boss adapted my job description so that I was writing training manuals rather than delivering training presentations. My friends and family took over household tasks I could no longer do. My church community prayed for me.

The biggest help came from my very wise therapist, Gloria. One day she said, "Gail, you are grieving everything you think you've lost. What do you still have that can help you through?" It took some time, but I finally realized I still had the power of my gift with words. The light dawned. Maybe I'd feel differently about my situation if I spoke about it differently—if I used my words not just to describe my reality but to define it.

Through trial and error and lots of talking to myself, I understood how to create change talk that helped me regain perspective and view my life through a different lens. Here are the principles of successful change talk.

### Principle 1 - Appreciate what you're leaving behind
Appreciate and honor what you're leaving behind, but don't cling to it. Recognize that you're not starting from zero when you're working to grow and change—you are starting from now and going to better.

### Principle 2 - Anticipate the successful change
Create a clear vision for how things will be once you've changed successfully. Believe in that vision.

### Principle 3 - Avoid comparisons
Comparison can put you in a position of judgment, lack, and negativity. Avoid comparing yourself to others, comparing then (past) to now (present) or when (future), and comparing perfect to possible.

**Principle 4 - Align your perspective**
Aligning your perspective means fully embracing the new condition or identity and accepting it as your own.

**Principle 5 - Acknowledge your authentic self**
Successful change must be consistent with your authentic self. Even if you do not initiate a change, ultimately, the change needs to be aligned with your values, mission, and message for it to be successful.

Over time, my condition has improved to the point that I only need oxygen at night. I can sleep in my adjustable bed, and I can once again get through a presentation without gasping for air. I'm certainly not back to the condition I enjoyed before my diaphragm became paralyzed. The most important improvement to my condition is the adjustment of my attitude—the growth in my ability to master change, whether it comes by choice or by chance.

I hope this checklist will help you to master change in your life as well.

# THE TOOL

Changes come into our business and personal lives by choice or by chance. You can choose to resist, merely accept, or master these changes. It's all up to you! While we sometimes think we use words to describe our reality, the truth is that words can sometimes define our reality. The language you use to talk to yourself and about yourself can make all the difference in successfully navigating a change in your business or your life. Follow the checklist below to become an A student in the process of mastering change.

## APPRECIATE WHAT YOU ARE LEAVING BEHIND

Appreciate and honor what you're leaving behind. Find a way to say "thank you" to your current situation or way of work for all it meant to you, and determine to take those positive aspects with you into your new life. Appreciate what you're leaving, but don't cling to it. Recognize that you're not starting from zero when you're working to grow and change. You're starting from now and going to better.

*Your Change Talk:*

- Speak from a position of power and control over your own process.
- Use language that affirms the motivation or reason for change.
- Acknowledge that change is happening.
- Talk about what has been good or what has worked.
- Name what you'd like to be similar or different in your new situation.
- Say goodbye to the past to make room for the future.

### ANTICIPATE THE SUCCESSFUL CHANGE

Create a clear vision for how things will be once you've changed successfully. Believe in that vision. Science tells us that the best predictor of whether you can succeed at making a change is whether you believe you can succeed. Remind yourself of past successes to affirm the possibility of success in the current effort.

*Your Change Talk:*

- Describe your ideal new reality in clear, concrete terms.
- Use words that affirm your competence and capacity.
- Eliminate resistance. Don't be a "Yabbit," always saying, "Yeah, but. . .".
- Say "When" rather than "If."
- Keep language future-focused.
- Name the benefits of your successful change as if they were already so.

### AVOID COMPARISONS

Comparison can put you in a position of judgment, lack, and negativity. In fact, comparison can keep you stuck and kill your momentum toward change. Here are three types of comparison to avoid: comparing yourself to others, comparing then (past) to now (present) or when (future), and comparing perfect to possible.

*Your Change Talk:*

- Avoid the use of "and" or "but" in describing your situation.
- Eliminate qualifiers such as "better than" or "as good as."
- Speak kindly to yourself through the process.
- Don't compare your "behind the scenes" with others' "highlight reels."
- Silence your inner critic and listen to your inner cheerleader.
- Redirect your attention when the temptation to compare arises.

## ALIGN YOUR PERSPECTIVE

Aligning your perspective means fully embracing the new condition or identity and accepting it as your own. It also means making certain that you're taking actions that clearly lead to the desired change.

*Your Change Talk:*

- Use language of ownership ("my," "our") to describe the new reality.
- Acknowledge that change can be hard.
- Describe yourself with a new "I am. . ." to reflect the change.
- Stop second-guessing yourself—no more "shoulda, coulda, woulda."
- Describe a changed state is consistent with your values, goals, and needs.
- Use "belonging" language to connect with positive, successful people.

## ACKNOWLEDGE YOUR AUTHENTIC SELF

Successful change and growth that can be sustained is change that is consistent with your authentic self. Even if you don't initiate a change, ultimately, the change needs to be aligned with your values, your mission, and your message for it to be successful.

*Your Change Talk:*

- Claim the change as chosen, even if it happened by chance.
- Make statements of commitment to the new reality.
- Avoid justification, rationalization, and explanation—embrace what is.

- Tune out nay-sayers—develop a script to silence them.
- Talk about the new reality as normal, not tentative.
- Be honest with yourself and others.

There's no doubt about it, change can be difficult. Make things easier for yourself by creating a positive internal conversation. You really can speak your way to successful change.

**Gail Dixon** is a speaker, author, and coach who guides people to hear and express the heart's voice that gives their life meaning and purpose. Gail is recognized as a top expert for speakers, thought leaders, and mission-focused entrepreneurs in creating messages that make an impact. As the leader of The Heart's Voice Movement, Gail is committed to creating a future where the Heart's Voice is the universal language that heals the world.

Connect with Gail at these sites:

Website: https://heartsvoicemovement.com

Facebook: https://www.facebook.com/gail.dixon.94

Facebook Group: https://www.facebook.com/groups/heartsvoicemovement

LinkedIn: https://www.linkedin.com/in/gaildixonmessaging/

CHAPTER 10

# TRUSTING SPIRIT

## AMPLIFY BUSINESS GROWTH THROUGH ANGEL CONNECTIONS

Rev. Mary Perry, Angel Intuitive and Healer

## MY STORY

In 1996, the angels came to me via my father, who had transitioned in 1995. My mind was heavy with sadness remembering that fateful day a year before, I wanted to feel my Mom's voice, so I reached out, and as the phone rang I heard, "Thank you for calling; there is no one here now to answer, please leave a message and we will get back to you." No big deal, except it was my father's voice.

We had recorded over his message the year before. Tears rolled down my cheeks: *I could not have heard that right. I must be imagining it.*

Dialing a second time, I heard my father's voice greet me, and this time I listened more than once to hear his voice. Tears streamed uncontrollably as I tried to pull myself together so I could go back to work. I felt like I did the day of his passing, devastated, and my insides shook as if I had been gut punched. I called a third time. I wanted to hear my mom explain how this happened, but she was coming from church.

"What did you do to the answering machine?" blurted out of my mouth.

"Nothing," was her reply.

She had a friend call, but that message did not play again. I recognized this awakening as the start of my sacred journey of working with my Angel Mentors. That message was mine, and I understood at a very deep soul level that this contact was to start me on my healing journey, healing from the childhood that was less than perfect, and to bring the angels into my life.

I can't wait to show you how you can connect with your Angel Mentors, too!

I explored—with great curiosity—classes, books, and channeling. In 2006, the angels stepped in and helped me start my business, now called Wings Unfurled. Yes, you heard me correctly—the ANGELS.

My corporate job was doing accounting for the non-profit American Cancer Society. Accounting was easy for me, but it didn't touch my desire to help people. I just knew my soul purpose was to help people. When I started, I felt the difference we made in local cancer patients' lives. That changed over time, and the company no longer served local cancer patients first. I was very grateful for my experience in Human Resources doing payroll. It helped prepare me for working with people. I treasure that, and yet, it wasn't enough. I wanted more. I kept asking the angels to bring me more. *Show me, help me, guide me.* These were my constant prayers.

My experiences with the spirit world grew, and I wanted to help people connect to their angels. *But how?* These words kept rolling through my mind. I meditate and journal daily, and my angels showed themselves through dreams, hawks, and feathers. I sat at my corporate office wishing I could work with the angels bringing them in by doing readings for others; however, I wasn't convinced I could do that as my main gig. I also bartended part-time at a local bowling alley. Not my dream job for sure.

One Friday night in 2006, I sat at a table in the bar waiting for the busy night to start and as I was reading my angel book I wrote, "I want to make my part-time money doing angel readings and healings." The night got busy and I threw the paper away at the end of the night. The next morning, a friend called to tell me of a store named Mystickal Voyage opening near our corporate office. On Sunday, I decided to see if I could find it. I tuned into my angels, and with two turns off the main road, I arrived. Okay, just so you know, all I had in mind was shopping. I had no idea shops like this would have intuitive readers. I loved being in this energy and looking at the oracle cards, books, and crystals, and I felt grateful for my angels guiding me there.

"I love your shop," bubbled out of me as I engaged with the owner, Lori. "So happy you like it; this is our opening weekend," was Lori's reply. I continued to shop and, at one point, heard another customer ask Lori if she would have intuitive readers. Wow, those words lit me up and opened my angels to start pushing me forward. I kept hearing: *Go tell her you do angel readings.* I couldn't continue shopping. The guidance was so strong I couldn't ignore it. I recognized that I needed to walk through the fear. *Can I do readings for money? Am I good enough? Am I ready?*

The angels' support quieted my fears, and with that, the need to voice the words about what I do wouldn't leave. Suddenly, I realized this was a pivotal moment in my life, and as I stepped into this portal of sacred energy, my mind filled with gratitude at seeing the realization of my dream and desires come to life.

I walked to the counter, and while trembling at the thought, my voice caught in my throat and the words, "I do Angel Readings," came out of my lips. Although the shop was very Wiccan and a bit different from Angels, Lori filled my soul with joy, saying, "Come do a reading for me and I will consider it."

I went back to my shopping adventure with my soul jumping for joy. As Lori and I talked, we formed a beautiful friendship that is still strong to this day. When I walked out the door, I called my friend; "I found a place to do my Angel Readings," bubbled out of me. Inside I was elated; my soul filled with excitement, and I jumped for joy! The next day I went back with my friend and Lori asked, "Did you bring your calendar so we can set times for you to read?" Surprised, I answered, "I thought you wanted me to do a reading for you?" Lori smiled and said, "No, let's just set times for you to come in." Through our connection, my angels helped her to see me! Don't we all want to be seen?

I began my new work life with my angels guiding me. My business name at that time was Whispers Through the Light, and in 2011, a meditation guided me to change my business name to Wings Unfurled. The angels showed me that my soul had unfurled her wings, and it was my time to soar. I checked in repeatedly to be sure and asked for signs and assurance that I heard them correctly and changed my business name. Wow, I was living my dream. No, it was not full-time, but it was fulfilling, and I gained so many connections and great experiences. My purpose and fulfillment skyrocketed, my confidence built, and more of who I was emerged. I began dreaming and visioning about doing this work full-time. Three years later, an opportunity presented itself, and I followed my angel's guidance to the next chapter of my work life.

I left my American Cancer Society job of 16 years to go work for an acquaintance I met in some of the angel classes I was taking. I managed her metaphysical store, worked in her corporate office, and did my readings and classes at her metaphysical business, Inspired Journeys. I was there until my corporate job with the company ended in July 2013, and I felt Angel's guidance to work my business full time. I heard that I was ready.

Over the years, my business has morphed and grown to where I am today. Along the way, I realized that being flexible with the guidance given was very important. Do not be led by your head but by your heart. Where you find your passion is important for all spiritual entrepreneurs. Passion gets excitement building in your soul and helps you step into your work. No matter what, my passion is the angels, and I love helping others embrace them and see, hear, feel, and know their guidance.

I have had many different versions of what my business brings to my clients, but the angels are always my base, and when I get confused, I go back to basics and the question, "Where do the angels want to help, and how do I bring that to the world?" fills my being. Then I listen for the answers, which come even if I don't recognize them at first. I trust that the angels and spirit always know what is best for me. They never say, "You *must* do this!" but rather, it comes more as an inspirational thought or feeling that sends me not from my head but from my heart. That is my treasure. My heart.

So here I am, 20 years into living my passion. I don't call it work because work feels hard, and what I do brings playing with the angels into the world. I believe that bringing joy into the world helps me cultivate joy in my soul garden. If my vibration brings healing, comfort, and joy, then I'm living my purpose. My angels told me that it's one by one that I will help others heal.

In 2012, I had a unique adventure on a Trinity Table that helped define my purpose even more as it took me into a deep meditation and life-changing experience with Jesus where I sat on his lap on a hillside under a tree and he worked on me, healing so much of the hurts that still resided inside me. Tears flowed, and I was sobbing with my body feeling as if it was shaking apart from my tears. As the healing subsided, I said to Jesus, "I don't want to go back." His reply still blows me away today and brings tears to my eyes. His words still fill me with the deepest wonder and awe, "You need to go back; you need to teach people about love." Being love, teaching love, and sending love to all are the foundations of my business. I understand that when that vibration leads me forward, people feel it deeply. It brings healing and puts love into our world.

I AM a healer of hearts who uses connecting without judgment to spread love to all!

One of my biggest treasures is my reputation. I relish that people connect with me. When I step into a session with someone, compassion and love lead me. The angels step in with wise words or teachings for my clients to help themselves. It's amazing.

One of my basic beliefs is that we can all do what I do; it takes a desire to look inside and do some of the more difficult work to change limiting beliefs or negative thought patterns. You may find different ways to connect with your angel team, but if you desire it, it's there for you. Are you ready to take your next steps? Let's talk about the angels and what your beliefs are about them. Can you trust that something outside your mind or control may be able to help you decipher what messages you get or that you get messages at all? This work can sometimes feel difficult, but I promise you that it's truly worth taking the deep steps to connect and follow your guidance. You are the wisest person you know! That wisdom lives deep inside, and that inner wisdom, along with your Angel Mentors, can be the most worthwhile journey you take in your lifetime!

## THE TOOL

My story is about trusting spirit, and I can hear your question: "How do I do that?" It's a valid question, and I know it takes time and a burning desire to work on yourself, digging deep inside. It takes working through limiting beliefs such as 'the dead do not talk' and 'angels do not leave signs of their presence.' You may need to work through old religious beliefs.

At one point in my journey, I posted signs saying "Trust" all around my home and car. One of my biggest laughs comes when a metal sign saying trust with a bell on it would ring when I was thinking something with my critical mind, not my loving heart. It was a great way for my angels to get my attention!

Let's set an intention that trusting spirit leads you forward. You may want to say or write this intention every day for a while. "Dear Creator, help me trust the support you send to me, and through these experiences, help me move with Divine Grace and ease in my life, trusting the Angel Mentors that step into my life so that I may experience daily guidance and love. Thank you!"

My second tool would be to recommend meditation. When I started, the "M" word created fear inside of me. *Can I stop this head voice and clear my mind? I can't do that!* At first, I fell asleep and sometimes snored during class when we were meditating. Did I let that stop me? No, I kept at it, trying different ways to meditate. I wanted to see, hear, feel, and know my angels. How does this help your business? Guess what? The guidance comes for business growth as well as your personal life. I wanted to fly in both areas, so I kept at it. Now I hold a meditation circle once a week. Meditation does not always bring instant guidance, but in the days following, it seems it opens channels for all of the questions in your head to find answers.

My gift to you is a recorded meditation. Build Your Angel Room is a place to meet your Guardian Angels and invite other angels to join you. The link to access this recording is https://wings-unfurled.com/angel-room/.

Reach out if you have questions about meditating. Meditating is a big key in connecting to your inner wisdom and angelic guidance.

Journaling is another tool that has always been helpful and crucial in living a joy-filled and loving life. Journaling takes that head voice, you know the one that brings up doubts and fears and helps heal them by emptying the mind so that guidance can imprint loving, inspirational new ways of walking your path. I always envision that I'm writing to Source Energy when I write in my journals. It helps remind me that I'm not in control of my life and that something bigger is afoot. Sometimes you may feel there is nothing for you to write. Ha! You can use journal prompts or affirmations, tell a story, or write about something that happened in your life. How do they help your spiritual business? Simple, as your words connect you to the authentic story of your life, your ideal client will connect by feeling your words. Journaling starts you connecting with your guidance and ends up helping you step into your soul purpose and passion. Try it!

It is sometimes easy to get lost in your fears and doubts. The more you meditate and journal you will begin to recognize when these pop up. They will come; please understand that is what happens as you step on this sacred path, for as you shift these thoughts, you'll find your soul expanding. When angelic guidance stepped in to shift this energy, I sometimes asked myself, *What if this happens?* Then I'd think of the response: *What if it doesn't happen?* As this becomes a natural response to those fears and doubts, magic happens. When the fear comes, find a minute to become still, breathe in love and create a new response. Feel the calm that takes over as the angels bring you to a new sense of self.

To find stillness:

Take deep belly breaths, pulling the breath of love deep inside you. As you release the breath, blow it out quickly. Concentrate on the breath. When the thoughts in your mind come, go back to the breath. Feel it going in and going out of your body. Feel how your body responds. After a few minutes, you find stillness, and then peace enters. Listen closely; this is where the magic happens. Tell your Angel Mentors that you're ready to see, hear, feel, or know their message for you. Take notice, come back into your body gently and easily, and write the thoughts that came to you in your journal.

One of the last tools is about understanding the signs that Spirit presents to you. Signs come in many ways, and as you begin this journey, they will appear when you're ready. As I write today, I notice a hawk landing in a tree outside my window. Curious, I ask my Angel Mentors what this means. *The hawk wants you to pay attention and be the observer. It comes at an important time in your life, inspiring your creative pursuits and awakening your vision.* If I hadn't noticed the hawk, I wouldn't have received this message.

Surrendering to Divine Source, I humbly and gratefully hear, know, see, and feel my guidance. I hear the inspiration to work with my clients to help them find this beautiful guidance for themselves. They guided me to develop the Discover Your Angel Mentors and Guides Program. The quicker you surrender to Creator or Source energy, the easier life becomes.

I lead a blessed life and I want that for you too!

**Rev. Mary Perry** is an Angel Intuitive and Healer. She brings her angelic touch everywhere she goes. She loves teaching others about angels through her business, Wings Unfurled, and brings this enchantment and wonder to you so you can move to your sacred self, embracing the world of angels and guidance from spirit. Living on the water in Sparrows Point, Maryland with her partner, Will, and cat, Luna, she enjoys nature and all the gifts it brings.

Her belief in magic and her connection to a world filled with angelic guidance, Divine Oneness, and high vibrational support enables her to bring to you messages of love and healing from the angels and your guides. This guidance is the basis of her inspirational, loving, and healing ways. With Wings Unfurled, she is dedicated to helping others connect to their inner wisdom and to walk their healing journey.

Rev. Mary Perry offers angelic guidance through Channeled Angel Readings, Seraphim Blueprint healing sessions, classes and Integrated Energy Therapy sessions and workshops, and her signature program, Discover Your Angel Mentors and Guides.

Rev. Mary would love to connect with you. Call or text 443-465-3060 or email Angel@Wings-Unfurled.com to connect.

Her website: www.Wings-Unfurled.com offers more information about all of her work and ways to work with her.

My signature program-Discover Your Angel Mentors and Guides, helps clients to develop a relationship with angels and tap into wisdom and guidance from their team of angels.
https://wings-unfurled.com/discover-your-angel-mentors-and-guides-program/

Angelic Care Calls – Complimentary 15-minute call to discuss whether we would be a good fit to work together. https://wings-unfurled.com/angelic-care-calls/

Angel Inspiration Circle weekly meditation circle. https://wings-unfurled.com/services/angel-inspiration-circle/

Facebook: facebook.com/WingsUnfurled
Facebook Group, Angelic Vibe Tribe:
https://www.facebook.com/groups/322780899221022

Instagram: mperry4372

CHAPTER 11

# YOUR ORIGIN STORY

## HOW TO BRING YOUR WHOLE AUTHENTIC SELF TO YOUR BUSINESS

Laurie Morin

Don't let anyone tell you that starting a spiritual business is a straight road. Finding your mission for becoming an entrepreneur is more like a winding country path with lots of detours and distracting scenery. But if you stay flexible and open to the unexpected, you'll end up with something greater than a business. You'll discover the joy in the journey and learn to flow with the current of the universe. This will lead you to your soul's purpose and the legacy you want to create with your services.

That is what happened to me when my business plans took an unexpected detour after retiring from my career at the end of 2019.

## MY STORY

I thought I had my transition from law professor to transformational coach all figured out.

For five years, I trained in all aspects of starting a coaching business. I had my certifications in hand, along with an inspired business plan.

When I retired, I planned to take a gap year, traveling around the world to scope out sacred and culturally rich venues. Then I'd launch my business by leading retreats to help women tap into their divine feminine power.

I thought this was the perfect business for me, combining my love for travel with my commitment to women's empowerment. But the universe had other ideas.

Maybe you remember the early days of 2020 as the calm before the storm. For me, it started with a phone call from my nephew, who was living with my 89-year-old mother in Massachusetts.

"Grandma says she is too dizzy to get out of bed," he said with a catch in his throat. I could feel his tears dripping through the phone. "I don't know what to do. She can't even get to the bathroom."

"Let me talk to her," I replied.

"Mom, what's going on?" I asked.

"Laurie, I'm so dizzy. I'm afraid to stand up because I might fall over," she whimpered.

I knew that voice. It was the same one she used when my father passed out on the living room floor, and she was paralyzed with fear. I had to call 911 and calm her down so she didn't have a heart attack before they got there.

"Okay, I will call somebody to come over and help you to the bathroom and then jump in the car and head up there. Why don't you have Nina take you to the ER, and I will meet you there."

I threw some clothes in a suitcase, said goodbye to my partner and dogs, and jumped in the car. It was 750 miles from our new home in North Carolina to the childhood home I grew up in, and I was determined to get there by the next day.

You can imagine the thoughts swirling in my head.

*I wonder if she had a stroke. Did her afib finally get her? Or maybe it's her lungs. The doctor said the COPD would get progressively worse. Will she make it until I get there? Is this the beginning of the end?*

On the road, I called my two younger brothers. They lived closer than I did, but it was still a hike for them to get there. My sister-in-law offered to make the two-hour trip to be there when my mother got to the ER.

By the time I got there the next morning, my mother had been admitted to the hospital and had every test under the sun. All came back negative. Her heart and lungs were okay. They had no idea what was causing the vertigo.

The doctors were ready to discharge her, but she didn't feel steady enough to go home. I tried to negotiate for a bed in rehab, but Medicare wouldn't pay for it because it wasn't "medically necessary."

When I told my mother the news, she was so distraught that I asked if she wanted to private pay. She had a bit of money from my father's life insurance, but I never thought she would say yes. Mom was the frugal one in the family, so when she agreed, I knew how scared she must be.

We found her a bed in a private nursing home nearby, where she received daily rehab and lots of attention from the staff. I visited every day, and my nephew got a much-needed break to visit his family in Vermont.

In the meantime, my business plans were on hold. I couldn't plan a retreat because I wasn't sure when I could leave Massachusetts. Then the other shoe dropped.

Slowly, the news dribbled out about this dangerous new virus that was lethal for the elderly and those with weakened immune systems. The nursing home started enforcing a mask policy and was on the verge of restricting all visitors. Just in time, I decided to have my mother discharged a week early against medical advice.

The day I arrived to pick her up, a big yellow sign on the front sidewalk said in bold red letters: "Danger, Do Not Enter." The front door was locked, and they were reluctant to let me in when I rang the bell. I told them I was there to pick up a discharged patient, so they let me wait in the entrance hallway while somebody went to get her and wheeled her out to the door.

Fortunately, Mom regained some of her balance and could get herself from the wheelchair onto the front seat of the car. She was sorry to leave the security of the nursing home but glad to be going home.

"I missed my house," she said. "All my memories and treasures are in that house. Please don't ever make me go to a nursing home."

*Shoot. She seemed so comfortable at Governor's Center that I was hoping she would be willing to consider assisted living. I don't know how we are going to keep this arrangement going. It's too much for my nephew to manage on his own, and we don't have the money to hire live-in help.*

"I know, Mom," I replied. "I will do my best to keep you at home, but you have to let me get you some more help. Is that a deal?"

We had tried to get some help with cooking and cleaning in the past, but she had always resisted.

"I can take care of my own house. I don't want anyone coming into my space and telling me how to do things," she'd protest.

This time she knew I had bargaining power, so she agreed to let me bring in an aide three days a week to help with light housekeeping, meals, and companionship and to give my nephew a break.

The next two years were a roller coaster of declining health, ER visits, and trips back and forth to Massachusetts. Sometimes I wouldn't even make it home before I got a call that Mom was in the ER again. We kept adding services—an adult daycare program for socialization, Visiting Angels for transportation, more health care aides to administer medicine and help with daily activities, and finally, a live-in companion to keep her company during sleepless nights.

When she got COVID at her daycare program, her decline accelerated. She started having hallucinations and panic attacks. When I wasn't there, she called in the middle of the night, terrified that kids on bikes were on her roof trying to break into the house. She called the police so many times that they refused to come to the house.

My partner and I started looking for a temporary place to bring our dogs so we could spend more time in Massachusetts, but before that happened, Mom passed peacefully in her sleep. I was grateful to be there and to see her long struggle come to an end.

In the meantime, between road trips, I tried everything I could think of to get my coaching business going. Planning events around my mother's caretaking was challenging, and international travel was pretty much shut down.

I must admit I sometimes gave in to the pity party in my head.

*Why is this happening to me? This is so unfair! This was supposed to be my time to travel and do the things that bring me joy after a lifetime of putting others first.*

I knew there had to be a lesson in the challenges I was encountering. I took up gardening, built a patio, and enjoyed afternoon drives to the beach to let the ideas germinate. But my heart longed for something more fulfilling. I knew so many women who were suffering, and I wanted to find a way to help.

I was resistant to the idea of taking my services online because I loved the deep connections and transformation you could create at live events. My business was pretty much at a standstill when I got a nudge from the universe.

*Remember that book you started three years ago at the Tom Bird retreat? Why don't you dust that off the shelf and finish writing it? Your experience recovering from a lifetime of people-pleasing could help a lot of women who are juggling the demands of work and family in these challenging times.*

Little did I know that was the beginning of the evolution of my business. I finished the book *Shero's Journey* and planned a retreat in Vermont to share the life lessons I learned with other women. To my surprise, nearly everyone who came to the retreat confessed that they had always wanted to write their life story. My book helped them see how that might be possible.

I heard the same thing from a group of women who agreed to be my beta readers. Many people on my mailing list wrote to tell me how much the book changed the way they looked at their childhood experiences.

All this feedback got me thinking.

I bet I could help women who want to write their life stories. I learned how to write mine the hard way, with lots of trial and error. I ended the retreat with thousands of written words but no idea how to organize them into a book. It was only when I discovered the s/hero's journey framework that I figured out how the pieces all fit together. I could help other women do that and finally write the book that is living inside of them.

So my new business model was born. I lead programs to help women bring their wisdom and experience to life in written words. In the process of writing, we discover our inner truths and heal old wounds. We write for our transformation but also to uplift and inspire other women on their life journeys.

So what does all this have to do with your spiritual business? I believe that starting a business, like writing a book, is a transformational process. You start with an idea, an inspiration, a nudge to your heart—but you can't know exactly where you are going to end up.

It's tempting to stick with your original plan, especially if you've poured lots of time and energy into it. But it's so much more rewarding to stay open to the gentle nudges from Spirit that may lead you in a different direction.

We have all heard how important it is to let our prospective clients get to know, like, and trust us. That means your business origin story doesn't have to be a perfectly straight line from start to finish. It can be a meandering path that shows your humanity and vulnerability.

That kind of story will attract exactly the right people who will be happy to pay for your services without any high-pressure sales tactics. Wouldn't that be a relief?

In the next section, I'll lead you through the process of writing a business origin story that you can use in the "About Me" section of your website, your full-length bio, or the introduction to a book showcasing your expertise and services.

# THE TOOL

Perhaps you've heard of the "hero's journey." It's a term popularized by cultural anthropologist Joseph Campbell in his book, *Hero With a Thousand Faces,* based on mythology and folk tales from around the world.

The hero's journey framework has been used in popular books and movies from *Star Wars* to *Harry Potter* to *Indiana Jones.* Campbell's student, Maureen Murdock, added a twist to the concept in her book, *Heroine's Journey.* She writes about the need to balance traditionally masculine values like power and worldly success with feminine values like love and compassion.

You can see glimpses of how those themes play out in the latest Wonder Woman movie. At the end of the movie, Diana realizes that war will never stamp out all evil. She vows that in the future she'll try to change the world with love instead.

When I was trying to organize the disjointed story fragments and ideas from the retreat into my first book, I figured, *why reinvent the wheel?*

So I combined elements of the hero's and heroine's journey to come up with my own framework, "s/hero's journey." I'm going to teach you a simplified version here to write your own business origin story in a way that will capture clients' attention and draw them into your world.

My advice is to answer these writing prompts as if you were talking to a friend about the joys and challenges of starting your business. The common wisdom is that our prospective clients are just a few steps behind on the same path we have followed. If you're open and vulnerable, they'll be grateful to learn from your experience.

- The Call. Where were you in your life when you made the leap to start your own business? Perhaps you were unhappy and looking for more fulfilling work. Or you lost your job to downsizing during the pandemic. Were you on a quest for money and power, or were you craving more work-life balance and fulfillment? Let your clients see that you've faced some of the same struggles they are dealing with in their lives.

- The Journey. Here is where you describe all the twists and turns and synchronicities that led your business to where it is today. Did you meet mentors and guides who helped clarify your vision? Did the universe put opportunities in your path that led to a bigger vision? This is an opportunity to let people see that you are doing exactly what you are meant to do to serve their needs.

- The Challenges. What obstacles did you encounter on your path, and how did you overcome them? Your clients aren't looking for perfection. They want to be inspired by your ability to overcome challenges to get where you are today.

- The Rewards. This is all about your personal definition of success. Have you achieved financial success and recognition? Are you happier with your life and more fulfilled? Let your clients know what you value most in life and how your services can help them live in alignment.

- The Lessons. Don't preach. Lead by example. Show your clients how much you've learned from experience and how you can help them avoid some of the mistakes you made along the way.

- You know how your math teacher used to say, "Show me your work." It's the same with your business. Don't just tell me your expertise. Show me how you got there. Make me believe that it's possible for me, too, and I will be your most loyal fan.

**Laurie Morin** is a writer, coach, and retreat leader who creates programs for women to turn their wisdom and experience into life-changing memoirs and nonfiction books. Her Writing for Empowerment community is a safe place to cultivate the inner writer in all of us.

Laurie is working on her second memoir, Chasing the 1970s, a coming-of-age story about her search for identity during turbulent times. The book will explore the parallels between the divisiveness of the 1970s and our current political and cultural landscape.

Laurie lives in Wilmington, North Carolina with her spouse and two fur babies. When not writing, she likes to walk on the beach, garden, and travel to cultural and sacred destinations. She has a white belt in Nia and is studying the ancient art of Qigong.

If you want to write your life story but don't know where to start, check out Laurie's free resources at www.lauriemorin.com/resources.

## CHAPTER 12

# ALLOWING THE AUTHENTIC YOU!

## THE SECRET TO ATTRACTING MORE CLIENTS

### Dr. Sree Meleth

## MY STORY

As I presented my offer—$2,297 for a ten-month Peace, Power & Presence (PPP) course—I could feel the energy drain from the room. Not a single person chose to learn more about the PPP. I was utterly deflated. *OMG, can I go somewhere and never be seen again?*

After nursing my bruised ego for a few days, I settled into my tried and true practice to find answers. After some mantra chanting, I started my meditation and inquiry. The question arose: *Sree, would you have spent the $2,297 for your course?*

*Of course not!* was the stunning response. Gobsmacked by my reaction to my offer, I went back through the process that had preceded the webinar and the creation of PPP.

I developed the course at the height of the pandemic. I recorded ten videos, and the idea was that this would be an evergreen course available on my website for $197.00.

I had everything planned out, and 2020 would be the year.

I went from full-time to two-thirds in my 9-5. I would get this evergreen course out, build up my coaching business, and gradually move to full-time coaching by the time I turned 65.

Then, COVID came. I was laid off in February. Because my skills are very marketable, I started a new full-time job on March 8. On April 2, 2021, my husband had a stroke. "Talk about a curve ball!" I muttered as my daughter and I changed and waited for the ambulance. This was not the first time life had thrown curve balls my way. They started coming at 19 when my mom, my closest friend, died in a plane crash on December 31, 1977. I hadn't fully processed that trauma, and this new encounter with the suddenness with which life can turn on a dime sent me spinning.

My response then was to not cry, take care of everyone around me, and immerse myself in life, including getting married and becoming a mom within two and a half years. Not surprisingly, my response this time was the same.

I became efficient. I had to change my routine. My husband recovered fully but was at risk. So I started commuting with him to Birmingham on Monday mornings and back to Atlanta on Thursday evenings because he worked for the Veterans Administration in both locations. This meant cooking meals over the weekend that we could use during the week in Birmingham and having meals ready when we returned on Thursday night. It meant struggling with attending meetings and learning to cope with the demands of a new job. Although I didn't realize it until I started writing this, I was seething inside. I had been through enough in life. It was time for life to go my way, damn it! I was damned if I would let life interfere with my plans again. I would go ahead and sell this damn course! *I dare you to stop me* was what I was saying to life, God, and the universe.

What does this have to do with the course and the webinar failing?

It made me unwilling to listen to myself. It made me say, "Screw you!" to the wise voice at my core warning me this wasn't it. *This does not reflect you or your value,* she told me. I was too angry to listen. I was also terrified of having to listen because that would mean I had to slow down, and then I would have to feel the terror, grief, and sense of abandonment I felt.

The anger and aggression I felt translated into actions like hiring a branding expert and listening to others about how I should market my course. This is why PPP went from $197 to $2,297. I was never comfortable with that price or the package. However, my refusal to listen to my inner wisdom and guidance meant I used a process and marketing strategy that felt utterly false.

I love my meditations. I'm proud of them. My message of learning to love and integrate the unaccepted parts of you into your heart and become a human being who is coherent and not scattered is invaluable. So, when I took the audience through the meditations and spoke to them about learning to love themselves, I was authentic and welcoming. However, as soon as I got to the marketing of the course, I felt icky. It was not valid. It was not me. My energy receded. As my energy left the room, so did the audience.

Many coaches would interpret this as me not valuing myself enough, not feeling ready to step up to my next level, etc. I respect that interpretation, but that was not it. I developed PPP during the pandemic as a tool, a gift to help the world calm down—to increase the number of individuals who have learned to love themselves unconditionally. I wanted it to be accessible to a large number of individuals. It was not conceived as a group course. It was supposed to be something other than a traditional group course sold the way so many coaches do. So, the way I agreed to market it was inherently false. My outrage at life and my "screw you, universe!" attitude left me vulnerable to being misled, albeit by very well-meaning guides.

What I needed to do was what I did after the webinar—use my tried and true practices to connect with my higher self.

First, I needed to stop resisting life (Tool 1). Second, I needed to take a breath and allow life to flow. Third, I needed time to acknowledge that it was terrifying to recognize that my husband and I were in the latter half of our lives. I needed time to feel all the regrets, the 'could have, should have,' etc., and process the grief.

I could've used the time to delve deep into the trauma of my mother's death. Looking at my husband, who had fallen on the floor and, for all intents and purposes, was no longer present for several minutes, was eerily like dropping my mom off at the airport and never seeing her again. Life had allowed me to work on a deep wound. Still, I pushed it away instead of welcoming it and decided to sell a new course.

The other important lesson here is that life has seasons. This was a time to feel my feelings, to use this curve ball to deal with the trauma of my mom's death and the fear of abandonment. It was time to reset, not to plunge into a massive marketing campaign. I refused to listen and used this campaign to stop myself from feeling anything too deeply. My alcohol consumption shot up after this, another sign that I avoided feeling anything too deeply. Honestly, I'm still dealing with the fear of what might be next. There is still much healing left to do. It takes a lot of letting life flow and surrendering.

I was not ready to stand before a crowd and sell anything.

I needed to stop and take a breath and let go.

Did that mean that I was frozen in time? Can healing and moving forward happen at the same time? Yes! It can. It's vital that we're fully present and conscious.

> What I have learned to do is to be true to myself.
>
> I get really clear about my values.
>
> I ask myself: What is my intention for the product or service?
>
> I ask myself: Who do I want to reach with this? Or who is my ideal client for this specific product?

I ask what feels right in terms of the price for this service. I ask the question that came up for me in my meditative inquiry - what would you pay for this?

If life has taught me anything in these past 64 or so years, it's that there is a time for everything to fructify. It's that I do best when I'm authentically myself. The trick is to allow time for an idea to ripen, be ready, and be satisfied with small steps toward the long-term goal. Since that webinar, life didn't stop. On June 30, I was fired from the job I started two months prior, a couple of weeks after my webinar!

Do you think life was sending me a message?

Several years ago, I collaborated on another book project called *The One Word Book*. Each author chose a word and wrote about the word's meaning in her life. So my word was *trust*.

My definition of trust is: Letting go, resting back, relaxing into the flow, knowing that life is always unfolding in my favor.

Given that definition, how did I respond to what, at the time, seemed like a failed webinar and my first experience of being fired from a job?

I finally listened.

I gave my dreams of coaching a rest. Then, I focused on getting a new job. That was the primary focus for now. I understood I didn't need to push as if I had no time left. I continued working on my book and published it in July 2021. I started a new job on November 1, 2021. Yes, I still have that job, and I love the support I have in it.

For my coaching, I have taken small steps that felt right and congruent. My guidance was to set the intention to be seen, heard, and valued in 2023.

On February 2023, I had my first book signing workshop; I restarted my podcast (This is Your Time to Shine) and have been invited to speak on several. I've been doing free Instagram Lives for at least seven to eight months. I've devised different ways to engage potential clients and feel relaxed and confident about where and what I'm doing. Most importantly, I am myself.

I do not regret having attempted the webinar then. I now know what not to do. I know to listen to the wise, quiet voice at my core. So how do you do that? Is there a way to get clear guidance? Yes.

> First, you get comfortable with where you are in life: Tool 1.
>
> Second, you spend time in silent, meditative inquiry to clarify your products and services, intention, and audience.

# THE TOOL

## TOOL 1: ALLOWING LIFE

This is another excellent practice to flow with life. When you are upset, for e.g., when I'm angry and resentful, using this practice transforms the energy, and the results are often miraculous.

1. What does the anger/resentment/grief/fear feel like (sensation, texture, color)?
2. Where do you feel this?

3. Scan your body and visualize the space where you feel this. Is there a version of you that you see there? Can you name what she is feeling by looking at her?
4. Take three deep breaths as if you're pulling air from the soles of your feet to the top of your head, and let it go with a sigh.
5. Sense or see a warm golden column of light at your body's core, starting at your crown, going through your heart, and in between your feet into the Earth.
6. Feel and see it expand; see your heart open with this column of light and let it envelop you.
7. Bring this sensation, the discomfort and agitation and the situation that is causing it to come and the version of you that is feeling it into this light as you say:

    "I am willing to feel this exactly as it is.

    I am willing to stop resisting this sensation.

    I am willing to learn to love this circumstance.

    I am eager to welcome the version of me that feels this

    discomfort into my heart."

    *Feel your shoulders relax; notice how you stop bracing.*

    *What you are learning to do is to stop resisting life. Making this a regular practice helps us relax into life and savor all of it, the crunchy and smooth parts.*

## TOOL 2- MEDITATIVE INQUIRY TO CLARIFY YOUR INTENTION, AUDIENCE, PRODUCTS / SERVICES

### MEDITATION, VISUALIZATION, JOURNALING:

1. Find a quiet place where you will be undisturbed and have a journal next to you.
2. Take three deep breaths. Visualize pulling air from the souls of your feet to the top of your head, and let go with a sigh.

3. Select a prayer or prayers that you feel comfortable with. This video ( https://www.youtube.com/watch?v=-byjrq-I0Go) is a great way to center if you do not have a prayer.

4. As the chant goes on, feel the vibrations, and sense the silence grow within you.

5. Bring the product/service you are creating/preparing to sell into this silent space, and let each of the questions below come into your mind and wait for an answer. Open your journal and let the guidance flow as you write without editing. Plan to repeat this meditation for each of these questions.

> What is my intention for this product?
>
> Who will this help, and how?
>
> Which of my values does this product represent?
>
> What is the highest price point that I feel comfortable selling this for?

Take time to get really clear. When you have the answers, imagine standing in front of a crowd and talking about your product. If it's right and ready and is truly who you are, you will feel the flow. Do not rush this. You will be ready when you are meant to be ready. Using these tools will help you get there.

**Dr. Sree Meleth** was raised in a Hindu Nair family by a devout father and agnostic mother. She was 19 and working through the teenage angst of deciding whether she believed in God when she lost her mother in a plane crash. With her mother, Sree lost her sense of home, her single steadfast source of emotional support and trust. A few months later, still bruised, shocked, and very tired of the back and forth in her mind about whether or not to believe in a God, Sree decided to try living as if she were a believer. Today, some 44 years later, that tentative step towards faith has blossomed into a steadfast knowing and unshakable connection.

That faith has stood her in good stead. Since losing her mom, Sree has experienced life in all its messy glory, from the devastation of loved ones committing suicide and falling prey to addictions to losing a child.

While moving across three continents and living in over 30 different homes, as her physician husband worked through post-graduate training, Sree raised two successful children and earned three Master's degrees and a doctoral degree. Additionally, she's a certified EFT(tapping) practitioner, the author of *More than Peace, Power & Presence through Meditation* (https://a.co/d/4eKMHTl), and developed a video course called Peace, Power, and Presence.

She has a podcast, "This is Your Time to Shine." She blogs and has published in The Elephant Journal.

She believes her purpose is to help clients drop questions of value and worth and stand tall, knowing they are invaluable human beings.

Connect with Sree:

https://www.instagram.com/freedomwithsree/
Free Tapping / Meditation Video every Thursday at 7 pm.

https://www.facebook.com/freeingourselves

Website:
https://freeingourselves.com/

Latest Blog Post:
https://freeingourselves.com/2023/04/30/stop-seeking-it-outside/

CHAPTER 13

# THE CONFIDENCE CONUNDRUM

## HOW TO CHANGE YOUR MINDSET TO GET WHAT YOU WANT

Jean Wright

A well-known speaker once said, "Confidence can't be taught, you either have it or you don't." I beg to differ. I believe having confidence comes from within, and it's up to each of us to nurture it and bring it out during our life's journey. Confidence-building challenges test us from childhood to adulthood. Once we recognize how those experiences can benefit us, we learn to change our mindset, allowing ourselves to bring to light our inner confidence to do the things we love.

## MY STORY

"You are so lucky to be tall," said my mother as I was standing on my tiptoes, reaching over her for a bowl on the top shelf of the cupboard. She always seemed envious of my height for as long as I can remember. Her challenges were finding clothes that fit her five-foot-four frame and being unable to reach things in high places. I guess I was living her dream.

Despite my mother's encouraging words to feel lucky about being tall, I always felt self-conscious. "Stand up straight," she'd say. "Don't slouch; you should be proud of your height." But what was my response? "Stop telling me that," I'd say defensively, growing tired of the reminders. Didn't she understand I just wanted to be at eye level with my shorter friends and slouching helped? She meant well, but I didn't understand.

I was always a tall kid, even in the third grade. The school photographer was directing us to stand in rows for the official class picture, his bossy, gravelly voice shouting, "Tall girls and boys move to the back row." I was already towering over most of the girls that year, some kind of growth spurt or something, and I didn't have to be reminded about it. I felt self-conscious.

Being in these awkward situations in those formative years, I got to know the tall boys, like Mark G. I guess you could say we became back-row photo buddies. We accepted our fate—always being shuttled to stand in the third or fourth row behind all the shorter kids. Only the tops of our heads poked out behind all the others seated or in full view of the camera in front of us. I thought the shorter girls looked so confident in the photos, sitting there on the folding chairs provided for them with their pretty dresses on display. In our row, only our heads and the collars of our shirts could be seen in the photos Mark and I were in.

And it wasn't always the chaos of class pictures that made me feel less confident about myself. Entering a classroom and viewing the desk set-up, I chose the one at the very back, knowing I wouldn't block anyone sitting behind me. How could I possibly sit closer to the teacher in the front row and not be in someone's way? "Please move your head," was directed my way by classmates behind me, which would be followed by self-conscious slouching. I could hear my mother's voice saying, "You're so lucky to be tall." How could she say that?

Being a tall child meant hearing comments about my long *flamingo legs* or *spider legs*, which accounted for most of my height. I also had to put up with my sarcastic uncle, who called me a *string bean*. I thought maybe there was something wrong with me. How could I be confident about my self-image, knowing I had what looked like flamingo legs or resembled a long green bean?

I had to learn that I should've felt confident about myself as someone who stood out, but I didn't feel worthy of that attention. I had to learn that my feelings about self-image would only improve if I took matters into my own hands and started using my height and personality to my advantage. Then, maybe I'd feel more confident about who I was.

Of course, my mother was trying to help me by being supportive in her way, instilling some sort of confidence by telling me how fortunate I was. I didn't recognize it at the time. She knew I had this confidence deep inside of me, I just had to reach in, take it out, and use it in some way.

Thinking back, maybe I started realizing I was respected for my height when I was asked to be the flag bearer as a Girl Scout in the Memorial Day parade. It was an honor to lead our troop down Main Street holding that flag in the holster around my waist, high above us, catching the wind and displaying proudly as we marched along. "You can do this," I was told by the leader-mom who suggested me for the job. What a confidence boost that was!

But how else could I use that confidence I found in myself to my advantage as I grew into an adult? How could I take my confidence to a higher level and earn an income while using it?

I was approached by my friend Rachel who sold kitchen products. She loved to cook, and so did I, and she had just started selling these products in people's homes. She said, "You love this line like I do, so why don't you join in and sell them too? I think you'd be good at it." I had never sold a tangible item to anyone except when I sold Girl Scout Cookies. *I told myself, she may be right; I love this stuff.* Rachel kept encouraging me, saying I could do what she was doing. She said she saw something in me, so why not? Could I use some of that inner confidence I knew I had to ask someone to buy something from me that I was passionate about? Whether this would improve my confidence or not, I didn't know, but I thought it was worth a try. So, I said yes. I bought into a home-based business model to get some confidence and make extra money for our family.

So, there I was, standing tall and proud in a stranger's kitchen, dressed in a crisp brown apron demonstrating a brand of cooking products. My presentation of the gooey and fragrant crescent roll pizza baking on stoneware in the oven for the past 20 minutes elicited oohs and aahs from the ten hungry ladies seated before me. Just before the reveal, I showed them all the kitchen tools any home cook would need to make this fabulous pizza creation. Instantly they knew that the simple techniques I showed them for making fun and easy meals would make them heroes to their families.

As I noticed how intently they watched me carefully cut into the crusty deliciousness using the oversized pizza cutter, I couldn't help but wonder how many of them were perfectly qualified to sell the products because they loved them as much as I did. I asked, "Don't these products make it easier for you to cook for your family?" Many of them, already fans of these high-quality items, confidently nodded in agreement. Then I asked more fervently, "Wouldn't it be fun to show your friends how easy it is to cook great meals using these tools and make money doing it?" Part of my job was to recruit new consultants to work under me, so I anticipated a resounding *yes* from the crowd.

Suddenly, the joyful thought of buying the products they loved and making their families' tummies happy turned into an uncomfortable recruiting sales pitch. I was not only asking them to buy the products I was demonstrating, but now I was asking them to consider selling them too.

"What? I'm not a salesperson," said the lady who said earlier that she'd love to make some extra money to contribute to the family income. "I could never do what you do," said the woman hosting us, who was literally caressing the mixing bowl she owned and passionately telling her friend next to her how much she loved the products. Wow, my first impression of them was confidence in themselves, and I couldn't believe their answers.

While these quality items sold themselves, which made my selling job a little easier, recruiting women to sell the products was much more difficult than I imagined. Why weren't they just like me? What was the difference between the two feelings of buying something they loved and selling something they loved? They *want* the product but don't feel confident enough to say they can *sell* the product. I could see they wanted to do it, but they talked themselves out of signing up.

So, what are the stigmas attached to feeling confident about what we can and can't do without getting down to our true feelings that we want to do it? What about saying, "I could never do what you do" to someone while deeply knowing you love everything about what they do but don't have the confidence to try it yourself?

# THE TOOL

When someone says, "I could never do what you do," is it a confidence issue? I always thought so, but often it reflects their admiration for your abilities or accomplishments. It's important to remember that each person has unique skills and talents, and comparing ourselves to others can be counterproductive. But how can we acknowledge this?

1. Express gratitude and thank the person for their compliment by acknowledging their kind words with a "Thank you, I appreciate that!"

2. Share your journey by talking about the hard work, dedication, and challenges you faced along the way to develop your confidence skills. This can help the other person see your success did not happen overnight and maybe feel more confident they can do it too.

3. Encourage and empower the person by letting them know they, too, can achieve great things with dedication and effort.

4. Help the person in developing their skills and working towards a goal. This can give them valuable guidance and support, potentially boosting their confidence.

Remember, when someone compliments you or expresses admiration for your abilities, it's an opportunity to be gracious, humble, and supportive. But it can also be an opportunity to show how much confidence you also have in them.

There are some things I decided a long time ago that I didn't want to do in life. These are non-negotiable occupations or activities that I know I don't like. I may have told a nurse, "I could never do what you do," because I won't administer a shot to someone or clean their serious, bloody wound. I don't *want* to do that, and I never will *do* that. But I appreciate her talents and skills for doing that job. I've told a friend who asked me to go hot air ballooning that I will never go up in a balloon because I fear heights, and it's not something I've ever wanted to do, and therefore I will not do it. There is no lingering desire there. But I appreciated their talent for piloting the craft and thanked them for offering me such a unique opportunity.

But what about those things we think we can do and don't try them? Why do we hold back from doing something because we have limiting beliefs that we can't do it? We may have a passion for something but talk ourselves out of trying it for fear of failure. Where is the confidence we need to follow through with our dreams, desires, passions, and hidden talents?

Changing your mindset about gaining confidence requires a combination of self-reflection, self-awareness, and consistent effort. There are steps you can take that will help you develop a more confident mindset:

1. Identity-limiting beliefs: Reflect on the beliefs and thoughts that hold you back from feeling confident. Recognize negativity and challenge them.
2. Set realistic goals: Break down goals into small achievable steps. This will help you build confidence as you see progress and experience success.
3. Practice self-compassion: Treat yourself with kindness, understanding, and patience. Learn to forgive yourself for mistakes and see them as opportunities for growth.
4. Surround yourself with positivity: Spend time with people who support, encourage, and inspire you. Do things that uplift your mood and make you feel good about yourself.
5. Develop self-awareness: Recognize your strengths and areas for improvement. Focus on your capabilities for progress rather than comparing yourself to others.
6. Affirmations and visualization: Use positive affirmations and visualize yourself succeeding in various situations to cultivate a more confident mindset.
7. Improve your skills: Invest time and effort into developing the skills and knowledge you need to excel in your chosen field or personal interests.
8. Embrace failure: Understand that failure is a natural part of learning and growing. Using setbacks as learning experiences can provide opportunities to improve.
9. Focus on the present: Practice mindfulness and stay focused on the present moment rather than dwelling on past failures or future uncertainties.
10. Practice confident body language: Stand tall, maintain eye contact, and use open gestures. This will not only make you *appear* more confident but can also help you *feel* more confident.

Remember, building confidence is a process that takes time and consistent effort. Be patient with yourself and celebrate your progress along the way.

Today, when I find myself in situations with friends and we're taking photos, I consciously choose to sit in the front of the group on the chair. I won't accept being pushed to the back anymore. If I had continued to stay in the back row and not had the confidence to say *I am somebody and I'm going to use my confidence to get what I want,* then I would've never known what it's like to be successful or to try something new. How do we, as women, not lose sight of our purpose? How do we change our confidence mindset to get what we want?

A confident woman embraces her inner strength. She radiates power to transform her dreams into reality, nurturing herself with courage, wisdom, and resilience. She becomes a purposeful woman who is fulfilled with the knowledge that she has overcome what has been holding her back. Instead of repeating the words, "I can't," saying instead with confidence, "I *can* do that."

**Jean Wright** is a Sales Confidence Builder and author of the book Selling Your Confidence: Forging a Successful Sales Career from Mint Cookies to Martinis. Her selling experience began as a young girl growing up in Pittsburgh when she persuaded her parents to allow her to sell Girl Scout Cookies. Her success in selling, which even impressed her parents, led her to pursue a four decades-long sales career. Jean has worked in sales and management positions for global companies, non-profit organizations, and media companies.

Jean's aha moment came when she was president of a women's business organization where she met sales entrepreneurs experiencing confidence problems. Her desire to help women raise their confidence levels inspired her to write Selling Your Confidence. Her career journey takes the reader on a path strewn with confidence-building challenges that many women may encounter during their careers.

Jean speaks to women's organizations and sales professionals about confidence building and has her consulting practice. She has two grown children and lives in Frederick, Maryland with her husband, Tom. She enjoys lemon drop martinis, visiting wineries, going to concerts and plays, and taking advantage of all that the Washington DC region has to offer.

To schedule a confidence-building session, visit Jean's website:

https://sellingyourconfidence.com/

To connect with Jean:

LinkedIn: https://www.linkedin.com/in/jeanwright-confidencebuilder/

Facebook: https://www.facebook.com/groups/sellingyourconfidence

Instagram: https://www.instagram.com/jean.sells.confidence/

CHAPTER 14

# CULTIVATING AN AGING SPIRIT

## THE HIDDEN POSSIBILITIES OF CHRONIC ILLNESS

Carla Johnston, DCN, MA, MS, CNS, LDN

*Might there be a way to find peace in aging? How might we find a way to cultivate an aging spirit? To create a positive experience amid a health challenge. Define wellness for ourselves in the face of challenge, to design a life of purpose so exciting that it drives us forward. Create and incorporate the concepts of **Both/ And**. To experience joy, purpose, and inspiration amid health challenges?*

## MY STORY

"I just want to feel better, to feel like myself again. It feels like I'm walking through molasses; the fatigue is ever-present, pulling me down. My calendar is chock full of doctor's appointments. I spend more time with doctors than my girlfriends." A short pause and sigh, "I guess that is just the way it is when you get older."

*Is it, though? Does it have to be?* I wonder.

Sitting back in my chair, I put my pen down slowly on the table next to me. I'm watching my client, now fidgeting with the tissue in her hands, nervously crumpling it and straightening it out again as she peers through the window over my shoulder. She seemed to be mesmerized by the drizzling rain on this damp, gray spring morning. She attempted to make eye contact, only to return her attention to mother nature and the soggy day outside. She has a few short bursts of energy as she continues to provide the details of her recent symptoms that led to the referral to my clinical practice.

She shifts in her chair; her left foot nervously moves from side to side. Visibly tensing and speaking through a clenched jaw, "It is not so distant a memory that I had a vibrant career. I earned the respect of my staff and team. We worked hard and accomplished many wonderful things together. Challenging, gratifying, and purposeful are all part of the workday. I was utilizing my talents and skills, boosting and encouraging newly acquired talent, and nurturing those with many years of service. It was sublime."

Another pause with a pronounced exhale, "Those days are gone. Now I feel old. My aches begin the minute I get out of bed in the morning, and my stomach hurts as the day goes on. There is just no relief." Her gaze shifted from the window to the floor. "I had visioned retirement as joyful and fun, a permanent vacation. I pictured myself going to lunch with my girlfriends, spa days, and traveling the world with my husband, channeling my inner child while playing outdoors with my grandchildren, and perhaps even starting a non-profit. None of this is happening. Doctors, prescriptions, constant blood work, lab tests, and referrals to additional experts. I live in confusion, as one expert's advice often conflicts with another."

"Do this and don't do that, eat this, don't eat that, get more sleep," she continued, her voice quivering and cracking, "and you should be keeping up your exercise to maintain your bones." Her simmering frustration bubbled to the surface resulting in a small tear in the corner of her right eye. With the motion of a ninja, she quickly dabbed it with the tissue—her constant companion this entire visit. She masterfully and skillfully wiped it away with a smooth and rapid movement. I would have missed it if it were not for my keen observation skills.

Then, Silence.

In the background, the faint awareness of the light rain continued outside—the gentle and rhythmic sound of tapping on the windowsill.

I purposefully didn't speak, didn't offer advice or consolation, no questions.

Just silence.

I wanted her to have this moment—a moment to breathe. A moment to process this conversation, let her know I was listening and that I heard her. There was no hurry, no need to rush through the visit. She had plenty of time to gather her thoughts, express them, and be with them.

This exchange was not a unique one. My clients often expressed similar frustrations, fears, and sadness. That aging was somehow something to 'get used to.' The best years were behind them; now, it was all about medicine and chronic illness management. As a clinical nutritionist, I often received referrals to work with those struggling with digestive (or gut) issues. Multiple clients expressed similar concerns beyond medical and physiological symptoms, experiencing emotional and mental health concerns such as anxiety, depression, and feelings of isolation. They were seeking assistance with managing both and looking for someone to listen to and help them find solutions.

These appointments began to shape my practice, as I had the opportunity to listen and work with those who felt alone, frightened, frustrated, and overwhelmed when they experienced health challenges. Most assumed, and had the expectation, that experiencing illness was an inevitable result of getting older, that they needed to find a way to make peace with it, and that it was unavoidable.

*Is it, though?*

I started asking myself profound questions about what I was creating in my business.

*How might I serve those seeking answers and expand the conversation from challenge and angst to questioning and possibilities in the presence of these chronic conditions?*

This curiosity led me toward continuing my education, resulting in my ability to provide a holistic, integrative approach to supporting health. Countless study hours steeped in botanical and traditional medicine resulted in academic knowledge, understanding, and achievement. I was amazed as I explored ways to merge this newfound data into a practice supporting those wishing to live well as they age. I became enchanted after reading about thousands of years of information and observation focused entirely on the body's wisdom and innate ability to move toward healing. For me, it was the perfect juxtaposition to conventional, contemporary medicine. The incredible gifts learned from thousands of years of traditional medicine alongside, and in tandem with, current evidence-based approaches to healthcare.

The influence of the mind-body connection is well documented and worthy of substantiative exploration. Digestive illnesses can often significantly impact mental health, such as anxiety and depression. Each can profoundly affect the functionality of the other. For example, I met a client with severe digestive symptoms and a recent irritable bowel syndrome (IBS) diagnosis. They were referred to me, by their doctor, with the request to provide a list of foods they should and shouldn't eat.

As is my practice, the conversation expanded, allowing time to share and process life's challenges. Through that exploration, it was a revelation to her that she was experiencing unexpressed grief. Our visits shifted to include nutrition education focused on digestive health, the influence of gut-brain communication, the benefits of mindfulness breathing activities, and the goal of attending a grief social group. I referred her to a therapist with specialized and extensive experience working with older adults and grief. Her healthcare team could now support her medically, physically, and emotionally. All of us focused on her overall health and well-being.

These experiences solidified my resolve to continue to have more significant conversations, not solely focused on good and bad or should and shouldn't. Exploration is essential when learning to experience the connection between thoughts and body sensations. This takes time, space, and breath. Not easily accomplished when rushed, in pain or discomfort, or when one feels dismissed or not heard.

Designing my practice was not linear—as the expression goes, two steps forward, three steps back. I spoke with a diverse group of successful practitioners who figured it out and followed their leads—utilized financial resources to attend many courses focused on practice creation and development. It was not easy; I struggled to find my voice and confidence. Attending webinars, weekly networking groups, marketing workshops, and hours spent reading articles and books for burgeoning practices seem to come together seamlessly one morning when describing my vision to my business coach.

*I believe my unique practitioner skills are working with those struggling with physical symptoms who feel that they are experiencing a loss of control of their health and life. We work together to broaden the discussion from a perceived loss of control to visualizing possibility, to find joy in physical movement, to experience passion when creating meals that nourish their body, and to shift from suffering and unhappiness to a sense of (new) control and enhanced engagement in life. The vision for my practice would be to be a resource for those making peace with where they are in the present AND to experience excitement about the future: a wholistic health practitioner and coach.*

Food and nutrition are undoubtedly significant influences on health and aging. I felt the need to expand the term *nutrition* to the concept of *nourishment*. What we put on our plates at mealtimes is essential; for me, so is what is happening in and around us. I wanted the conversation to expand from only looking at one's meal plate to *nourishing what's on life's plate*. It allowed for deeper conversations and exploring one's challenges and goals. I have found that providing education on the digestive system's influence on overall health is incredibly valuable. Most are fascinated to learn about the microbiome, gut-brain communication, and the impact of sleep on the gut, to name a few.

Our uniqueness invites us to reflect on these influences and adapt accordingly. Food choices influence our health, especially as we age. And I submit that if one is not living the life they imagined or having difficulty with a life transition such as retirement or even the loss of a partner, or the addition of a medical diagnosis making life challenging- the conversation and exploration needs to go beyond "eat this, not that."

That is the practice I created, providing space to create a fulfilling life in the presence of these conditions. The flexibility and possibility of Both/And.

*How would I adapt the concept of **Both/And** into my new practice and business? What would be a first step to acknowledge that I have the experience and vision in the face of doubt and fear? Am I willing to concede that I have trepidation and still move forward? That I can be afraid **and** tenacious? That I can feel stuck **and** still move ahead?*

This concept of both/and has played a significant role in my personal, academic, and professional life. It has allowed me to experience that everything is on a continuum, dynamically moving and that nothing is static. There is a wisdom to aging with countless opportunities to continue learning and growing. Challenges don't necessarily negate happiness or joy. Anxiety doesn't cancel out laughter or amusement. All are part of life and health- both mental and physical – mind and body.

Learning is a process whether you wish to expand on your success or create new habits. Having the tool of exploring your *Both/And* can assist you in cultivating possibilities. Acknowledging what is and what you are moving toward is often helpful, even in the face of upset, discomfort, and challenges. What is your *Both/And?*

# THE TOOL

## MINDFUL EXERCISE: CREATING YOUR *BOTH/AND*

Take a moment and find a quiet, comfortable place to sit. For those who find it helpful to write things down, having a journal or clean pad of paper could be advantageous.

- Close your eyes and take a few breaths.
- Feel the chair supporting you as you breathe in and out. Allow your thoughts to float as if on clouds in the sky: no judgment or commentary. Just notice your thoughts.
- No 'right or wrong'; stay present and notice your breath. If your mind wanders, it will just let it go.
- Begin to cultivate thoughts of gratitude. What is going well in your life? What are you grateful for today? This moment?
- Take another breath and enjoy the feeling of sitting with gratitude.
- What is it that you desire to do? What are your plans and goals?
- Continue to breathe. In and out, observing these thoughts as they float by.
- No judgment or critiques. Just breathe and what you want to move toward.
- Take a moment to visualize your *Both/And.*
- Allow yourself to stay in this space with breath and calmness, allowing all thoughts to float by.
- Take a few breaths and bring your attention back to the room.

- When ready, open your eyes and move your body gently in your seat. Move your feet, hands, arms, legs, shoulders, and head slightly.

For those who wish to write in your journal, note things you want to remember or critical observations you wish to keep track of. Notice how you feel after this exercise.

An example of a *Both/And* mindful practice:

> "I am experiencing a loss of appetite and intense stomach discomfort after eating, causing me to feel isolated. I want to be able to socialize with friends yet feel challenged by an intense fear of going out to enjoy meals with my friends. I feel self-conscious and embarrassed, so I stay home."

The goal is to be able to go out with friends, enjoy social connections *and* be mindful of symptoms. The *Both/And* exploration begins with acknowledging, with gratitude, that friends are understanding and wish to be supportive.

> How can you have *Both* social connections *And* do so in the face of fear?
>
> Some possible areas of exploration:
>
> What may be possible if you discuss these concerns with your practitioner, therapist, family, or friends?
>
> How might some possibilities be created when openly discussing it with supportive resources?
>
> How supportive would it be for you to host a get-together and share your goals, plans, struggles, and challenges?
>
> What might asking for help look like for you?
>
> How can you take a small step toward your plan, goal, and desire?

The purpose of this exercise is to create possibilities for yourself. One of my favorite quotes is Emily Dickinson's "Dwell in Possibility." And I have often tasked myself with my quote, "Insert Confidence Here." Not everything begins with confidence, especially when we are learning. Take a small step forward and keep going; confidence often follows action.

It takes practice, patience, skill, and tenacity to build skills. Allow yourself that. Be kind to yourself and give yourself the same grace as a dear friend. Calm the judgment voice and breathe.

I plan to be *(Both)* a lifelong learner and *(And)* adapt to these learning lessons as I move through life. I embrace aging and look forward to this journey. I am mindful to remain focused on mind-body-spirit.

How about you?

**Dr. Carla Johnston** is a board-certified nutrition specialist and certified health coach. She earned her Doctorate in Clinical Nutrition and her M.S. in Herbal Medicine from the Maryland University of Integrative Health and an M.A. in Applied Sociology from the University of Maryland, Baltimore County, where she focused on the impact of chronic illness on aging adults.

Carla is a practitioner and a passionate advocate for those wishing to incorporate health-positive behaviors and partner with those seeking to live their best lives as they age dynamically with grace and purpose.

"Merging the wisdom of traditional medicine and contemporary evidence-based practices allows for a deeper understanding of ourselves. Designing a unique approach provides a rich tapestry of potential opportunities to shift our ideas, choices, and goals." Through the lens of many influences on health, which she calls the Nourishment Nine's, she works to expand and deepen the conversation, exploring mind-body connections. Her Nourishment programs focus on creating an individualized approach to whole-body-centered health and supporting those wishing to experience Aging in Health, Purpose, and Grace.

Carla co-authored a best-selling book, "Called to Lead: Successful Strategies for Women" focused on providing insights and guidance for women in leadership and released her first book, "Freshman at Fifty: A Story of Dreams, Determination, and Self-Discovery" detailing the journey toward goals of life, during times of struggle, obstacles, and challenges.

Dr. Johnston's next project is creating a membership program for individuals in their 60s, 70s, and 80+ who want to thrive, grow, and embrace life, regardless of age. Members will share challenges, insights, and successes, unlocking possibilities that NOURISH their lives. Weekly discussions, and guest speakers, will focus on topics such as nutrition, movement, social connection, health challenges, and life's purpose.

https://www.drcarlajohnston.com
https://www.facebook.com/drcarlajohnston
https://www.instagram.com/drcarlajohnston
https://www.linkedin.com/drcarlajohnston
https://www.youtube.com/@drcarlajohnston

CHAPTER 15

# DREAMING THE IMPOSSIBLE DREAM

## HOW PRAYER WILL TRANSFORM YOUR MIND AND HELP YOU THRIVE IN LIFE'S TRANSITIONS

Olivia A. Jones, Independent Beauty Consultant, MPA

## MY STORY

*If you allow fear to overshadow your dreams, you will never try anything new, create anything new. Worst of all, if fear causes you to retreat from your dreams, you will never give the world anything new. When leaders are no longer willing to dream, it is only a short time before followers are unwilling to follow. So, dream! Dream big. Dream often. Somewhere in all those random ideas that your mind has is one that will capture your heart and imagination. And that seemingly random idea may very well evolve into a vision for your life and leadership.*

~ Andy Stanley

Janet Jackson said it best, "When I was seventeen, I did what people told me. Did what my father said and let my mother mold me." At seventeen, my father instilled in me my first life's mantra. It was a statement written in the Cattellian booklet for the 1987 Debutants for North Florida Chapter of the Charmettes, Inc, a local civic organization in Tallahassee, Florida. My dad wrote, as I began a new journey in life, that Olivia Jones (that'd be me) would pass this way and touch the soul of man. Life has given me some curve balls. I've had to endure challenges like everyone else. No one is immune to pain. Yet, I have dared to dream.

The Poet Langston Hughes said, "Hold fast to dreams for if dreams die, life is like a broken-winged bird that cannot fly."

In my early twenties, I decided I wanted to become an entrepreneur. I graduated from Florida A&M University with a degree in Broadcast Journalism. I wasn't sure what was next for me. Upon obtaining my undergraduate degree, I temporarily relocated to Philadelphia, Pennsylvania. This was a new adventure for me, something I'd never done before.

*Can I make this move? What will it be like living in a big city?*

There was a vision before me, and I decided I was up for the challenge.

A few months after making the move, I was invited to breakfast in Valley Forge, Pennsylvania at a five-star hotel. The memory is crystal clear, as though it just happened yesterday. On a crisp fall Saturday morning in 1993, I attended a Mary Kay breakfast. In the parking lot outside, there were pink Cadillacs and red Grand AMs. Inside, the women were dressed to the nines, and the energy in the room was electric. The food was delish—grits, eggs, and bacon.

The Mary Kay ladies looked like celebrities, and the aroma of their perfume was hypnotizing. The experience was enchanting. I sat there with a full belly. I was completely enthralled. Yes, I was in my happy place. The Mary Kay women shared their reasons for joining the company, which ranged from earning additional income, receiving recognition for a job well done, earning the use of a car, tax advantages, and being their own boss. The ladies shared heartfelt stories which solidified the company's underlying motto of Love, Leadership, and Legacy. Women who were living the dream. Sabrina Godwin Monday's story stands out to me.

"I started my Mary Kay business single with no children, and now I'm married with three children. I really love being home and having a business where I can spend quality time with them and be involved in their school activities," shares National Sales Director Sabrina Godwin Monday. She feels enormous pride when she sees her business principles filtering down to her children. "They know how to praise others, give recognition, and set goals. It's really a wonderful thing."

Sabrina says she's changed over the years, and she is happy with the person she has become. "I think the Mary Kay opportunity has given me permission to be me. When you're in a newsroom, you can't be who you want to be. Editors have their own ideas of who they want you to be and how you should fit into the mold. My Mary Kay business celebrates me for who I am."

At the time, I found myself at a crossroads. I wasn't sure what to do with my life. I had three choices. The first choice was to go home. Second, go to graduate school, or third, get a job. As I was thinking to myself, a woman turned to me and said, "You should do this."

So, on that cool crisp Saturday morning over bacon and eggs, I received the answers I needed, and at that moment, I decided to journey down the road of entrepreneurship. It was the best decision I've ever made. The decision provided answers and a way to make new friends and develop new skills. I could return home to Florida and help my mother, who had taken ill. The business was a source of unlimited income. I enjoyed the flexibility of being an Independent Consultant. I was given the opportunity to learn while I earned. I even began to live out the philosophy of God first, family second, and career third. It was instilled in me that in that order, life worked, and out of that order, life did not work. When I applied this philosophy, I found it to be true. I had no idea I would embark on a journey of self-discovery that would last a lifetime. Nevertheless, I decided to act on my dream.

The courage to dare to dream! Tenaciousness became my second nature, for there were myriad obstacles I faced that seemed to defer the dream. There were times when business was good and times when it was challenging. One of the most challenging times was at the height of the 21st-century pandemic.

The pandemic was a time of swift transition. One minute everyone was experiencing day-to-day living, and the next, there were quarantines, wearing a mask was required, and loved ones were dying; the business world experienced a major blow. The economy seemed to be operating at a snail's pace. Even grocery shopping was impacted; we had to shop in designated directions, which felt awkward.

The world, it seemed, came to a complete stop. The way business was conducted changed in the twinkling of an eye. Remote work was common. Businesses had to create a new way to serve their clients and customers. The trending term for the workplace was "The Great Resignation."

As a home-based business owner with Mary Kay Cosmetics, it was challenging to determine how to make my business work. I was accustomed to interacting with customers face-to-face and building a relationship where they could get to know, like, and trust me. Social distancing required individuals to stay six feet away from others. Network marketing taught us to warm chatter with anyone who came within three feet. Ugh! My fear factor went from 0 to 100 immediately.

*I don't want to contract COVID or infect anyone with COVID. How am I going to market my business? Will I be able to find business partners?*

There were all sorts of concerns, which were overwhelming. As a result of all the uncertainty, anxiety was at an all-time high for everyone. I clung to the scripture, "Be anxious for nothing, but with prayer and supplication, make your request known." As I laid out my request, pivoting became a way of life.

*This, too, shall pass! Keep going and growing.*

## THE TOOL

Ultimately, dealing with change can be challenging, but using prayer as a tool helped me ease the process. I took a moment to reflect and ask for guidance. My self-talk went something like this: *Trust in yourself and the path that is meant especially for you. Remember to take things one step at a time and have faith that everything will work out in the end.* It could have been easy to focus and dwell on my fears; instead, I chose to look inward and pray.

## PRAYER – THE CATALYST AND INSTRUMENT TO A NEW WAY OF THINKING AND LIVING.

My prayers are most honest when I'm all alone, just me and the Lord. I feel secure. I'm in my safe space without judgment and condemnation. During the onset of the pandemic, I was at a crossroads and struggling with a new way of living.

The struggle was real. Gradually my dream became elusive. Self-sabotaging thoughts such as *I am not an achiever,* and *life has seemingly dealt me a losing hand* dominated my thinking. I continued to pray. *Why would I be given a dream and no ability to make the dream come true? Is this a cruel joke the universe is playing on me?* Absolutely not. I needed hope. As I prayed, I began to have hope and a belief in the impossible. Sarn Kiekegaard said, "Hope is passion for the possible.

As the world changed, I didn't believe I could succeed in business. The harder the struggle, the harder I prayed. There were times it appeared as though my prayers weren't being answered. I was giving one hundred and ten percent, and the return on my investment seemed like negative fifty. So, I went into my secret place, my private closet, and made supplications for divine direction, protection, and provision. Slowly doors began opening. Confidence and clarity blossomed from within. I changed. Prayer made the difference for me; it helped me discover my purpose and calling. The good news is that the practice of prayer can transform your life, too.

I had limiting beliefs about finding customers and clients.

*No one wants to buy skin care! I can't do this.*

I bought into the limiting belief that I didn't know how to sell. I doubted my abilities even though, as a Girl Scout, I learned entrepreneurial skills. I knew about setting goals, doing presentations, money management, etc. Yet, I found I didn't truly believe in myself. The cassette tape (I grew up in the eighties) was playing in my subconscious mind with the recorded lie that I couldn't achieve the life of my dreams. Yet, instead of shrinking back, with a new-found confidence, I was determined to grow and move forward to become the best version of Olivia so that I could make a difference and pass this way and touch the soul of man.

What did I do? Although I had gained a new level of confidence, the battle to see my dream come to fruition was still intact. I prayed more fervently and consistently. I prayed with other like-minded individuals. My prayer life was orchestrated into a scheduled time. A personal prayer space was created for me to become quiet and alone without any distractions. There were no cell phones, idle conversations, or overthinking. It was a time to listen for answers to my supplications, specifically as they related to my business. Additionally, I created a gratitude journal, acknowledging daily my appreciation for everything that was happening for me. Writing five to ten gratitude statements every day helped transform my attitude.

During and after those prayer times, I began to relinquish control of the outcome of my efforts for my business. My struggles with how others perceived my success turned into confidence, especially when I stopped comparing myself to anyone who achieved greater success. Comparison created depression. My steadfast prayers and determination turned my depression into joy.

There were numerous obstacles to endure during the pandemic, such as how I would find new customers and how I would service existing customers. I was guided to my purpose and calling. It's been said there are two important dates in life: "The two most important days in your life are the day you are born, and the day you find out why." – Mark Twain.

## SURVIVING AND THRIVING IN THE VIRTUAL MARKETPLACE

There were other business owners who needed to learn how to run a virtual business too. While networking and doing research, information was obtained on how others were keeping their businesses afloat and pivoting, which provided direction.

*My business may not be able to survive this.*

Self-doubt would try to creep in. Yet, I continued my supplications. My support system helped me create win-win solutions. We prayed collectively for our businesses. I collaborated with a similar business hosting a virtual Lipstick Flirting Master Class, which accelerated my confidence. This business venture allowed for fun and education on lipstick application and the fundamentals of flirting. I reframed my thinking; the pandemic closed the world and opened it up simultaneously.

## LITTLE PRAYER, LITTLE POWER, SOME PRAYER, SOME POWER, MUCH PRAYER, MUCH POWER.

I was a winner no matter what. My self-confidence and belief in my abilities began to override my limiting beliefs. I kept showing up and praying. When my mother was ill, the business provided a strong support group to help me through the difficult transition of not physically having my mom with me. I always knew she'd live on within my heart. I began to actively pursue the changes I wanted in my life, like stability, freedom, and fun. I desired to be free to develop personally and professionally. I added another life mantra: When you change the way you look at things, the things you look at change.

When I recognized a skill or aspect of someone I liked and wanted to acquire, I began to study and practice the skill. As a result, my skill set grew. I wasn't a good planner. I sought out individuals who were planners. I read books on planning. Planning was implemented into my daily routine and schedule. Organizational skills were developed. I started hanging around people who were good organizers. My communication and leadership skills were improved by becoming a member of Toastmasters. Also, earning a Neuro Linguistics Practitioner certification helped put me in a position to break through my limiting beliefs and ascend to another level of living. My circle of friends changed. There were more balcony people in my life. My prayer life became more specific. I asked for clients who had a need or problem I could help solve.

## GOD ANSWERS KNEE MAIL WHEN GOD WINKS, MAGIC HAPPENS.

Discouragement turned into encouragement. Why? Simply because I prayed. I prayed often, consistently, in public and in private, and most of all, I prayed. God answers. The universe answers. Talk to your higher power, your God, your creator. Take time to connect with your divine source. You will find direction, protection, and, perhaps, correction.

I found magic. My steps were orchestrated by a loving heavenly father concerned for my well-being. My business did a 360 turnaround. My online clients increased. I begin attracting a new caliber of business partners. I became a new person. The Olivia on March 18, 2020, was not the same Olivia on March 18, 2023. I was changing. I was purged. Old habits and old ways of thinking were dispelled. As my needs were being met, I began to see the needs of others met. Little did I realize that who I had become was an answer to someone else's prayer. Prayer is powerful. Prayer is effective. Pray. Pray often. Pray when business is good. Give thanks for the provision; enjoy the moment. Pray when business is bad. Remember, it's only temporary. Tough times don't last; tough people do. Pray fervently. Pray and wait. Wait for your answer. Pray and act. Pray and believe. There is peace when you pray. There is strength when you pray. There is power in prayer. You'll be amazed at how you will experience a radical transformation in business and life; you will witness the ugly, gnarly caterpillar turning into a beautiful, bright butterfly.

**Olivia A. Jones** is a graduate of Florida A&M University, earning a B.S. in Broadcast Journalism and an advanced degree in Public Administration. She has held a variety of positions and roles, including writing tutor, adjunct instructor, and administrative assistant. One of her most rewarding roles has been as an Independent Beauty Consultant with Mary Kay Cosmetics. She has been a part of the Mary Kay team since 1997. She has been a Team Leader, Star Consultant, and Miss Go-give recipient. She enjoys being a consultant because it gives her an opportunity to help other women develop self-confidence and self-esteem, and she can live her life according to her values and beliefs.

In her spare time, Olivia enjoys spending time with her dog Beasley and other relatives and friends, volunteering with Toastmasters International, Girl Scouts, and the North Florida Chapter of Certified Public Managers Organization. She has recently taken up the challenge of learning the game of chess.

You can connect with Olivia and to learn more about opening a home-based business visit: www.marykay.com/oajones Facebook groups at https://www.facebook.com/groups/thepinkpamper or linked in at https://www.linkedin.com/in/olivia-a-jones-206a6426/

## CHAPTER 16

# TIME TO SHOW UP

### IF NOT NOW, THEN WHEN?

Gurpreet Juneja

## MY STORY

I was forced into it. It was a choice I made so it would stop haunting me. The most challenging part was that my new business was nothing based on my skillset, education, or the expertise I acquired over the years; instead, it was utterly the opposite, based on my intuition.

As I roll my MacBook cable and put it in my laptop bag, I see a brown-haired young man walk into the classroom with two of his friends. They were sitting next to each other, conversing and sharing thoughts in the first row of my session that I just ended. *They might have a question for me.*

I pause and look at them. "Can I help you?"

"We enjoyed your session today," the young man says, smiling and shaking my hand. "The insights you shared opened my eyes and taught me something about myself that I never knew. Thank you for a great session."

"Hi, I'm Dan, and I would also like to acknowledge how inspired I am by your talk today. I have never felt this optimistic about my life; I feel like capturing this moment and setting some bodacious goals for myself. Thank you," the second young man standing next to us expresses, with a hand over his heart.

"You have no idea what you have given me today; the third one exclaims, smiling at me. The session with you was by far the best investment I've undertaken in myself. Could we please get a picture with you?" the young man asks.

These words from these young men have moved me. As I leave the room and walk across the Gaylord Rockies conference room, other young professionals show their respect and gratitude towards the insights they gained in my sessions on change management and holistic leadership. Their words, smiles, hope, and desire to shake hands and hug me show the value they received from the workshops. My heart swells, and I remind myself, *Isn't this the reason I started all of this to begin with? To bring real change into people's lives, show them their own power, and help them lead their lives as successful leaders?*

It was not an easy path from where I started, but we must follow our dreams, find our true purpose, and live the life we desire. And that can only be achieved with patience, persistence, and being bold enough to listen to our callings.

I didn't think of having a business and running my own workshops. I had a very successful job, a well-balanced life, and a beautiful, loving family, and I made sufficient money to meet all our necessary and not-so-necessary needs. I loved having all the free time I had. Why would I want to add something else to my life, especially something that would bring so much ownership, accountability, and, most importantly, vulnerability into my life?

The drive to create a new business was beyond the analytical mind; it came from a much deeper place. I tried to shut it down many times, but it only got louder and louder. My left brain and right brain were fighting for their rights of who would own the heir of this kingdom and lead in defining what my life would look like, and neither one was ready to give up.

We all are here for a purpose, to add and give something to this world that is unique to us since we're all so different yet one at the same time. I feel called upon to serve a bigger purpose. I was at a place where the Universe showed me my purpose; trust me, it wasn't all clear in one go. I didn't see the entire path, but the signs came as I hiked the dirt road climbing up the mountain on a cloudy, windy day.

*Starting something new is always daunting as an adult. What is the world on the other side? Getting out of your comfort zone, becoming your own boss,* *following your dreams led by your heart, and stepping into another world…*my mind questions it all.

*I have done this before, not once but many times; why is it so difficult this time? Why can't I be curious enough to discover what's on the other side? What will it take me to get out and be bold, create my place in this world, and be loud enough for others to hear me? What is stopping me from showing my own true, authentic self?*

A small trembling voice in my head is scared to jump off the cliff and be vulnerable in front of the whole world, showing the real me.

*How can I do that? What if nobody likes the authentic me?*

And then I hear another much calmer voice, the voice of my heart, asking: *Why does that matter?*

*Wait what? Why does it matter if anybody likes my authenticity or not? It makes me vulnerable; I expose myself to people only to discover that I am not accepted. Why would I do that?*

This inner dialogue keeps growing. The fight between my creativity and analytical abilities, the heart, and the brain, doesn't stop and keeps getting stronger daily.

*How do I settle it down? How do I make peace with it? I'm searching for inner peace here; what will bring that to me?*

And my heart responds: *Only by sharing your story, being authentic, and owning up to all you learned in this life. It's straightforward to say one makes mistakes, but what do they bring? They bring a deep sense of learning, which made you who you are today; you are a living example of your mistakes. And the only way you will find peace is by sharing your journey, the ups and downs, the rivers, and the valleys, both the sunny days and the cloudy long cold bone-chilling nights.*

This interaction with myself keeps propelling and pulling me into the oceans of inner wisdom. Every day it asks me a bigger, bolder question, almost pushing me closer to the cliff's edge.

MY HEART: *So, you ask why I would make myself vulnerable without the reassurance of acceptance? Do you accept yourself as who you are today? Do you embrace your truth fully and unconditionally? If you do, why do you seek approval from the outside? What would that bring to you anyway, besides boosting your ego? I'm not asking you to work from the ego mind; that's what you have done for many years, making a living using your analytical brain. Do you understand what door needs to open to unleash all that you have within that is yours, with a unique signature, offered to this world by you?*

MY MIND: *Okay, I don't understand what all that means; where do I start, how do I go about it, and what do I do?*

MY HEART: *Now, you are talking. Leave all that to me; your job is to focus on your authenticity because the moment you lose that, you lose me, and I am your guiding star. You don't need any world-acquired knowledge or skillset. You need to hear me, and I will lead you to your true power by tapping into the infinite wisdom you hold within yourself through your connection to this Universe. Mind you though, one thing I warn you about is that it won't be easy, it's way more than getting out of your comfort zone, but it will be well worth it. Because tapping into your true power will show you how you can help others to do the same, and there is no more significant power than that, and even better, no bigger purpose than this,* the heart claims.

MY MIND: *Got it, so what do I do now? Where do you want me to start?*

MY HEART: *Well, wait for my guidance. As I said, I will show you the trail step by step, curve by curve; look for the signs and follow them. Sometimes you may run into the attraction of the other trail; every course will lead to a different path; it's your choice which one you want to get on.*

MY MIND: *Wait, how would I know which one would lead to what? How would I know if I am on track?*

MY HEART: *Oh, you will see if you are on track or not, if you are anchored to me and can hear me; you may not know which sign leads to which way, but it will resonate with you, and it will be loud and clear. You must be very present and an active listener to carve out your unique journey and not give in to your unconscious thought patterns,* my heart warns. *I am not going to lie to you. It won't be an easy road, but you can take my word for it that every step you take toward any sign I show you will bring you a deep sense of satisfaction and fulfillment. And that ultimate true living will be full of fun and adventures, making you feel alive again.* My heart exclaims with excitement.

MY MIND: *But what if I step away from the trail I should be on and head out on a track not meant for me?*

MY HEART: *Every movement I show you will be a growth path in some fashion or form. The track, not meant for you, will bring a different gift; a lesson of taking a step forward will follow through and bring you back the way you should be going. And remember, there are infinite possibilities on how you get to your destination, but the key is to make the journey worth living, and that's what I am offering you.* My heart sounds like a friend I can trust my life with.

*That's a lot to take in,* my racing mind thinks. The ego mind's job is to be the devil's advocate to protect me from any foreseen danger, which can bring danger, maybe not physical but emotional or mental.

I can't process all this very quickly. How can I rely just on my intuition coming from my heart that much when my mind can't even comprehend it? Oh well, I can ignore it for now and not do anything about it. I am not denying it anymore, but also not ready to embrace it all just yet. It's okay, I tell myself.

But that's not what the Universe holds for me. It's another day, and I'm going about my day, and here it comes again.

MY HEART: *When do you plan to start on this journey with me? I know you want it.* The heart questions like I owe it an answer.

MY MIND: *I am still determining when. I would like to know if I can or should.*

MY HEART: *Don't fool yourself. You know you can; you know it very well. Only when you can align your intentions with your actions you can do it, and do it marvelously. Are you questioning your existence? We all have a unique signature, a unique existence on this planet. We can choose to be part of a herd or find our true purpose and serve humanity and other life forces based on what we came here for to begin with.*

It keeps prodding me.

*You have been crushing me and ignoring my voice for all these years. What excuse do you have now? You are a mature woman, with all your needs met from a societal perspective; now what is stopping you? Do you want to find out what you bring to this world in your unique way? Or do you prefer wondering for the rest of your life?"*

The voice is not only annoying but getting louder and rude.

MY MIND: *What is my life all about? Was it to gain the worldly skills to make a living, get a car, a house, and make a family? Was that it? Or was there a bigger purpose to my life, something more and beyond me? What if I was here to help humanity in some way, bring some change in my own unique way?*

MY HEART: *You are okay with not moving forward, being stagnant water in a pond, staying warm and cozy, predictable, polluting the environment, prone to developing social, emotional, and physical problems, becoming a breeding ground for nuisance around you, rather than being a river that flows, a force of change for better, cleaner, healthier living, being a support system for a flourishing ecosystem?* It pops its opinion again with much more assertiveness.

MY MIND: *Be a river? Do you understand what you are asking of me?* I question with confidence.

MY HEART: *Yes, it goes through some mysterious paths, runs down from the mountains, becomes a waterfall, and there are fluctuations; you are in the unknown, not knowing what comes next, but there is movement. The river is flowing and growing with life to be where it belongs, and in this journey of self-exploration, it experiences the natural, vulnerable beauty of life. Are you sure you don't want that?*

My inner talk pushes me hard, and I step out into the unknown and embrace what life has to offer as I pave this path of self-exploration. On this transformational journey, there's a significant perspective shift. It's a consistent work on how I look at life, its events, different situations, and variations. What does movement mean to me? The medicine I offer here is a part of the new perspective I acquired as I started flowing with life. I cannot say I've mastered it because I'm scared and get nervous at unknown signs and paths, but the tools listed here give me a bigger perspective and an authentic way to work with my limiting thoughts and beliefs. I refer to these as ever-evolving go-to mantras, and I use them to carve my entrepreneurial journey to keep me in flow, conveying the reasons why I'm on this journey in the first place.

# THE TOOL

## IF NOT NOW, THEN WHEN

Being a flowing river makes you vulnerable, but here are some ways to help navigate the rapids as the water currents rise.

### 1. Opportunity for Growth with Size and Complexity

As I started flowing with the waters of life, I realized I was learning something new with every step I took. It felt like being young, alive again, and life was teaching me a whole new meaning of everything around me with a different lens every time. Listening to my inner voice opened so many doors of possibilities, and I found myself growing, not just vertically with worldly knowledge, but inter-dimensionally. The union with the Universe showed me how much there is to experience.

### 2. Discovery and Exploration

Just as the river flows through unknown territories and discovers new landscapes, being in the unknown can be an opportunity for exploration and discovery. It allows us to see things from a new perspective and discover new passions, interests, and opportunities we may have overlooked due to our environment or limiting beliefs.

### 3. Building Resilience

Stepping out of our comfort zone into the unknown allows us to overcome fear. Facing our fears frees us from our judgments, building our resilience towards what we define as our relative success or failure. It allows us to go above and beyond our physical bodies, exposing us to the larger world beyond our visual one.

### 4. Seasons and Stages

Just like rivers, human lives are also shaped by our environment. Rivers mature with different seasons and stages, contributing to a larger ecosystem. Exposing ourselves to the unknown gives us an opportunity to advance as we maneuver the different seasons and stages of our lives, making us experience life in an expandable way. Ultimately, recognizing our connection with the world around us can help us to live a more meaningful, responsible, and fulfilling life.

**5. Ecosystem Interdependence for Sustainability**

Embarking on a journey that drives your passion inward is a calling not just for you to awaken to your true purpose but also for those you are here to serve. If not for yourself, then embark on this new journey for those whose lives you will touch and most likely change in a better way. They all count on you for their sustainability. Be a Statue of Liberty to show them the light you carry.

**6. Embracing Innovation and Creativity**

A river embraces all it encounters, expanding and enlarging as it moves forward. As we flow with life and open ourselves to walk through the doors of varied opportunities, the key to innovation and divine creativity is right behind those doors. What we create through these opportunities is the unique signature of our existence, just like our biometric footprints and DNA strands.

**Gurpreet Kaur Juneja** is a multifaceted practitioner, encompassing roles as an holistic transformation life coach, speaker, certified NeuroChangeSolutions consultant, author, and emotion and energy healer. Her compassionate support extends to young individuals, men, women, and parents who find themselves challenged by the stresses of life and experiencing burnout. Gurpreet offers both in-person and virtual healing and coaching services, catering to individuals and groups.

Operating under her business CosmoBeing, Gurpreet provides a diverse range of offerings including custom designed programs, webinars, podcasts, and interactive workshops centered around promoting a healthy and joyful lifestyle. These experiences equip participants with practical tools for profound transformation from within. The term 'cosmo' symbolizes our infinite potential as beings, encapsulating the wisdom of the Universe within ourselves. It also serves as a reminder of our interconnectedness with everything around us.

Gurpreet serves as a channel for divine essence, aiding others in establishing a connection with their soul and nurturing unconditional love for all on this magnificent planet, Gaia. As a wife, mother, and holder of over two decades of leadership experience in the tech industry, Gurpreet has discovered true joy, peace, and ecstasy by following the divine energy residing within her heart. Her mission is to ignite this inner fire in every individual, enabling them to tap into their authentic essence.

With an unwavering commitment to personal growth, Gurpreet operates as an agent of change, dedicated to inspiring others to maximize their potential both personally and professionally. She encourages clients to break free from limitations, expanding their imagination and expectations of themselves. By transcending their perceived boundaries, individuals can unleash their true potential.

Gurpreet's soul finds harmony in connecting with Mother Earth. During her leisure time, you will find her hiking or driving through breathtaking sun-kissed mountains, meditating beneath the starry night sky, or passionately preparing vibrant meals using fresh vegetables from her own backyard, infusing each dish with vitality.

Connect with Gurpreet:
Website: www.Cosmobeing.com
Facebook: https://www.facebook.com/iamacosmobeing
Instagram: https://www.instagram.com/cosmo_being
LinkedIn: https://www.linkedin.com/company/iamacosmobeing

CHAPTER 17

# FILL YOUR WELL

## USING ART, BEAUTY, AND NATURE FOR INSPIRATION AND PEACE OF MIND

Melissa Harris

## MY STORY

"You can live with nothing, but it has to be pretty nothing."

Those were the words of a psychic palm reader I consulted with in my early twenties. That statement continues to hold. I've lived in places such as a tenement building where I could see through the ceiling of my bathroom up to my neighbor's apartment and in a shack on a Mexican beach. The common denominator is always *beauty*.

I painted and carpeted that tiny New York City tenement apartment all purple—my favorite color then.

In that apartment, I created some of my most imaginative oil paintings and pastels and an essay strong enough to have me chosen for a prestigious Fulbright Grant to paint in Paris.

I've been fortunate enough to have been able to make my living as a visual artist and writer since I was in my early thirties when I started my publishing company Creatrix, publishing my first greeting cards, followed by other items with my imagery. To make this happen, I needed quiet, comfort, natural light, and beauty to get still enough inside myself to listen to what wants to emerge. That still place inside of us houses the truth of who we are and stores the wealth of gifts we have to offer. My space can be messy, tiny, or very old, but it needs to contain those elements to allow me to reach my inner well.

## WHY FILL YOUR WELL?

Occasionally life can feel flat and dull. You know those times when you find yourself unmotivated or blocked? Trying to paint at times like this does not serve me. I can procrastinate for hours, clean up, or mess with my phone, and by the time I have to leave, I haven't accomplished a thing. I can't force inspiration.

The feedback I often receive about my art is that it carries energy. If I'm not feeling much emotionally when I go to paint, the effect of that lack of excitement about my subject will reflect itself in a mediocre piece of art.

In the same way, you will draw new clients and customers to you when you share your enthusiasm about your offerings. In quite a few instances where I've been very engaged with my work, I'm joyously dancing around to my favorite tunes when I'm painting while someone is contacting me to purchase a piece of my artwork. I believe that this joyous energy expands outward thereby attracting potential interest in my work.

# THE TOOL

## IDENTIFY WHAT FILLS YOUR WELL

It's human nature to respond positively to beauty. Beauty is easy to find in nature, but loveliness exists in unexpected places as well. Beauty could be the shade of violet in a friend's dress or how light falls in a tiny apartment at a specific time of day. Beauty can be the notes a favorite singer reaches in a song or the feeling or visual a piece of writing stirs within you.

In recent years I have found I need to be near the water. If I'm having a down day and go for a swim, the whole world can turn around! A fellow swimming enthusiast once exclaimed that she could solve the problems of the world after a good swim. I can understand why she says that. I love floating on my back when I swim in my nearby lake so that I can see the clouds above and hopefully catch a turtle resting on a sunny log or spot a heron. All of my senses are engaged. I might hear the various bird calls, smell the mossy earth, feel the silkiness of the water on my skin, and of course, enjoy the beauty of the trees and grasses nearby.

Have you heard the term "like attracts like" or seen the film *The Secret*? I used to visit stores across the country to do what I called Spirit Essence Portraits. During a portrait visit in a store in Florida, I met a woman in the store who would be doing a presentation that evening. If I meet someone or come across something that could be significant in my life, I get strong signals informing me of the importance of the individual. I might see a kind of light around them or feel excited in my solar plexus. I saw a glowing light shimmering faintly around the woman in the shop in Florida, and even though I was tired, I attended her talk. The discussion resonated with me, and I ended up back in Florida three weeks later for a weekend training on manifestation which turned out to be a turning point in my life. The training taught me how to become aware of what I am feeling and how to keep my feelings positive as I move through life.

By staying in an open positive place as much as possible, *your* well will be open to bring you inspiration.

An acquisitions editor for Llewellyn Worldwide Publications discovered my art along with the first book I wrote at a Natural Living Expo, and she felt that I was a perfect candidate to write a book on the connection between creativity and spirituality. I was honored to accept the offer. I had a difficult time getting started on the project, not because I lacked the content. I just found myself staring at the piles on my desk, getting distracted, and I couldn't access what I needed to express in that environment.

I needed to take my desktop computer to a friend's husband for repairs. While dropping it off, I observed my friend at work on her laptop in a light-filled area of her den in a comfy recliner with a steaming cup of tea. That "light" went off inside me again. Her workspace looked so cozy and inviting. I wasn't comfortable sitting in front of my desktop computer in my dark, cramped, and uninspiring office space. When I returned home, I went about creating my own optimal area in which to write. I decided to use my laptop instead of my desktop computer and situated myself in a recliner where I could see a pretty area of my yard. I made it a point to show up daily at the same time with my cup of tea and begin writing, no matter what. I looked forward to sitting in my comfy sunny spot, and eventually, I got into the flow.

I invite you to consider the teachers you've had in your life. Did any of them spark something that made you want to pursue their offerings? If so, how have you been able to implement these gifts?

I had a painting teacher who must have woken very early to drag all sorts of props on the subway from Manhattan to Queens, New York. She created fantastic colorful surroundings to situate our model in. It worked in that it made me want to capture that beauty on my canvas.

Her painting style was impressionistic. Her discussions about impressionist artists were full of enthusiasm about that particular style of painting. Often after these discussions, I couldn't wait to get to my easel. Her enthusiasm for painting contributed to helping me formulate my style of painting.

## GO OUTSIDE

Nature uplifts me any time of day.

It's predictable.

I get that afternoon slump every day, anywhere from two to four. Walking outside no matter what the weather jump starts my system and cleans me out so I can start fresh. A favorite exercise is observing the same tree daily to look for changes. Leaves can be blossoming or slowly dying. Birds may be nesting. Tree branches may have fallen. Another one of my favorite nature outings is visiting a nearby reservoir. The color of the mountains behind the Reservoir can change tremendously in just one hour.

Maybe you are someone who enjoys gazing at the night sky. Do you have a feeling of excitement in watching the sun rise or set? Perhaps gazing out the window at a snowstorm invigorates you. I'm fortunate to live in the Catskill Mountains, where I can be a part of the four seasons. Oddly, I find myself inspired to work on dreary days. A particular kind of peace comes over me when I know I can't be out of doors gardening, but I find the cloud formations lovely in their way too.

Nature feeds my soul. If you don't live in a rural environment, parks and botanical gardens can do the trick.

## TRY FENG SHUI

I've had someone practice Feng Shui in two of my different homes to help bring in changes. I had positive results the first time I hired someone to do the practice. The practitioner instructed me to place uplifting art about the house and to hang paintings with particular themes in specific spaces. In the bedroom, if one wants to bring in a relationship or celebrate an existing one, the images should have twos in them. You could place a painting of a couple in nature or two swans on a lake, etc. I realized that all of the paintings I hung were of a single woman, and I wanted to call in a partner, so I made those changes, and voila, my partner appeared.

Feng Shui also works with creating abundance, so if you want to bring in more clients, you can make your home and office spaces more attractive while also manifesting more business.

Feng Shui is too broad of a topic to delve deeply into for this writing, but knowing that you can use color, live plants, artwork, and much more to build an environment that will foster your business.

## TAKE AN ART COURSE OR GO ON A RETREAT

I teach Art and Spirit workshops both in person and online. Sometimes people want to attend but have no art experience and are afraid to take a chance. I hope what I'm sharing in this chapter will help you follow your heart and heed the call for what calls to you if this feels like you. In my destination retreats, I witness attendees blossoming in ways they would not have predicted. I know this from their feedback afterward. They have let me know that their experiences have been life-changing:

*"No matter what I do or where I go, I will always remember such joy is just simmering beneath my surface."*

*"The time in Ireland was life-changing for me. I was opened in a way I still do not completely understand. I feel a 'power' flowing through me that I no longer question. I feel more connected to those around me because of a 'knowing' and I feel a strength that I have never felt before."*

*"Visiting that last stone circle was both life-changing and life-affirming, a gift from the goddess and all the women that came before. The retreat was a reminder of the importance of being open to the universe, of ritual, and of gathering and sharing space with those we were meant to know."*

When I felt a bit "dry" and needed a significant change in my environment, I registered for a safari to South Africa. The safari nor the location had been on my bucket list, however, a peer who was born there presented the offering, and I knew it was a unique situation that could be a real adventure, so I signed up and was well rewarded. When I first read her announcement about the retreat, I felt that familiar excitement in my solar plexus and, after some deliberation, decided to take the leap and join in. I returned feeling strong because I had taken a risk to travel to someplace I was nervous to visit. I saw wild animals on their turf, which deeply touched my heart. I take my paints with me everywhere I travel. I was watering at the mouth to paint the gorgeous warm earthy tones of the landscape. When I sit and paint "plein air" (on-site), I can meld into the environment, taking in not only the sights but the smells and how the ground I'm seated on feels different from the grass back home. My well feels full. In South Africa, I enjoyed using different colors in my palette. This is exciting for an artist!

Of course, traveling across the globe is not something one does weekly, so I look to local opportunities when I need to switch things up and fill my well.

Dance and musical concerts excite me. I am a frustrated dancer, but besides being amazed by how the dancers use their bodies, the costumes inspire me. Sometimes clothing can create interesting shapes for paintings. I take photos at performances and use the photographs as jumping-off points in my art. I may insert a figure in a posture from one of the dance photos into a landscape painting, but I've even added a figure to a finished landscape!

Concerts inspire me differently. I often have visions that lead to ideas for painting while listening to music. These visions come from varied music ranging from Led Zeppelin to classical to Hildegard of Bingen. My imagination travels on the rifts of songs into mysterious places I might not ordinarily access. I'm eager to paint when I return from a concert.

## MEDITATE

I'm not consistent with meditation, but when I am meditating regularly, I feel a difference. I reside in the right side of my brain during meditation the way I do when I attend a concert, and this relaxed, receptive state relaxes me. The practice of meditation is another way in which I receive visual images, and they come unexpectedly. Occasionally, I also receive helpful insights.

When I meditate, I begin with a declaration of gratitude, usually followed by some form of breathwork. Breathwork helps to calm my mind and also helps to bring me fully present. I might then create an intention or ask for help with a particular issue I'm addressing. Upon sinking into a deep meditative state, I relax enough to let my thoughts dissipate. The visions can come or not!

I've experimented with taking this imagery I receive and creating small watercolors or charcoal pieces. If I like these studies, they earn a larger surface, paper, or canvas. You might try sketching what appears after you meditate, even if you do not have art experience.

## THE BEAUTY OF DREAMTIME

Dreams are another tool I rely on for direction and guidance. I record them, even in the middle of the night, and do a dream analysis with each one. I took a couple of dream workshops during the Covid years, expanding my knowledge to understand how to interpret them. The process I studied helped me make some relatively big career decisions that year. In addition to gaining a deeper understanding of my unconscious realms, sometimes the dreams provided intriguing images that I wove into my art. I keep a visual dream journal where I do pen and ink and watercolor sketches of the visions that inspire me. Colors may be more vivid; landscapes may be more fantastic in dreams. It's fun to attempt to put these ideas down on paper or canvas.

## IN CONCLUSION

Familiarity with what fills your heart and soul will help to keep you inspired and ready to fill the wells of your clients/customers. When you radiate joy, others around you will respond in common. Even a simple smile is contagious. Try that out on your next grocery outing! I like to envision helping others to feel peaceful when they engage with my art or writing. We're all each others' teachers in so many different ways. Your gifts will inspire others in ways you may not conceive of when you feel happy and fulfilled. An appreciation of beauty can be contagious. I hope the tips here will help you find or expand your sources of inspiration that you can pass on to those in your circle and beyond.

**Melissa Harris** is an internationally published artist, author, and teacher of art and life. She holds a BFA from Syracuse University in Painting and an MFA in Painting from Queens College. She received a Fulbright grant to study painting in Paris when she was 30. Her art and writing include:

**Books:** *99 Keys to a Creative Life* (revised in 2021 as *100 Keys to a Creative Life*) *Painting Outside the Lines*

**Card decks:**
*Anything is Possible* activation card deck
*Goddess on the Go* by Amy Sophia Marashinsky and Art by Melissa Harris.

Melissa facilitates Art and Spirit Workshops and retreats at her Catskill Mountain studio in the US, Italy, and Ireland. She helps participants find their unique expression by combining painting with meditation. The gatherings lead attendees to create new art tribes and artwork they're proud of.

She shares her home with her partner on nine acres in the Catskill Mountains of New York. Her land has beautiful grassy meadows and a magical forest that back up to a reservoir, complete with an organic garden and fire pit.

Sustainable living is at the top of her list of priorities. "I feel an obligation to live as simply as I can with an awareness of how each action is related to the next, both in terms of how we can be as waste efficient as possible, and also how we relate to others."

"Painting is my medicine…Through these decades of a sometimes erratic and ever-evolving life, painting had been the one constant. Relationships and homes have come and gone, but my paint box is always with me." From my book *Painting Outside the Lines.*

www.melissaharris.com

www.mharrisfineart.com

Facebook: https://www.facebook.com/profile.php?id=100063593086010

Instagram: https://www.instagram.com/melissaharrisart/

Pinterest: https://www.pinterest.com.au/mharrisart/

Youtube: https://www.youtube.com/channel/UC_OlTLzl90RRANOv_Ajo21Q

## CHAPTER 18

# SEE YOURSELF AS ANGELS SEE YOU
## SUCCEED IN YOUR SOUL'S PURPOSE

Lilia Shoshanna Rae

## MY STORY

What if we could see ourselves as angels see us? Would we then feel unconditional love for ourselves and the world? Would we be able to shine our light more brightly and succeed in our soul's purpose?

### YOU ARE LOVE

A dear friend, highly respected in the intuitive healer community, asked me, "Who do you know who truly loves themselves?" I looked at her quizzically because she would have been the first to come to my mind. "What do you mean? Don't you truly love yourself?"

She sighed and said, "No. Not really. And I can only think of one person who does."

This caught me off guard, yet I realized I was in the same boat. I was hard on myself. I knew how imperfect I was. I struggled with self-love even as I yearned for love from others. My angels tried to get me to know myself as love since my midlife encounter with them. It was a tough sell. I knew too well my flaws and foibles. I didn't feel deserving, and my heartbreaks were proof.

My angels didn't give up. They kept reassuring me. "You are love. When you know that and know it in your bones, your gut, and every cell of your body, you will exude that love for yourself and anyone you encounter. You will change the world by solely doing that."

Only in the last few years have I come to know the power of accessing what is already deep within me. My angels finally got through to me, and as I listen to their guidance and see myself through their eyes, I discover a whole new way of being. I create more of the life of my dreams for my family, friends, and beyond.

So how did I get here, and how can the lessons I learned help you manifest your visions for your life and the world?

In my search for love, my heart was broken big time. I also broke a few hearts along the way. I kept asking, "What is love? Will anyone ever love me? What do I want as love?" My life was like the song from the sixties, "Both Sides Now (Clouds)" by Joni Mitchell, seeing love from both sides and still not knowing love at all.

The heartbreaks I had as a teenager when listening to that song were nothing compared to those as an adult—a divorce after a ten-year marriage with my children's father and then a breakup and betrayal by someone I identified with as a soulmate. He chose my best friend instead.

Then my angels intervened. I was in my mid-40s and mid-career as a lawyer.

At that point in my life, I didn't know angels talked to humans. I thought they were historic creatures honored in biblical stories teaching us in the same way as stories about Noah, Moses, and Jesus. Little did I know that a broken heart would open me to their loving presence.

When my soulmate left me for my best friend, I felt a gaping hole where my heart was supposed to be. It felt like a cannonball hit me and obliterated the space between my breasts. I could hardly breathe, let alone do my work as a lawyer.

One day on my lunch break, I took a walk to clear my head so I could function. I had my job to do, three young children to care for as a single mom, and a life to live. I was desperate to heal this hole in my heart space.

It felt like the final nail in the coffin of my heart. *I must not be lovable if even my soulmate doesn't love me.*

And then I saw something on my shoulder. It had a voice. I turned my head over my shoulder in both directions to see if anyone was near me. No one. And the voice said, "It's okay. You're going to be okay." These words seemed to be coming from this being who looked like a little guy dressed in a suit, wearing a fedora. I thought I had lost it—first my heart, now my mind.

"Don't worry. It's okay. You're hurt, but it's going to work out. You feel unlovable, but you are loved. In fact, you are love."

At this point, I couldn't let him keep on. I felt I was going off the deep end. I interrupted and asked, even though I felt crazy as I was asking, "Can you tell me who you are and if you have a name?"

He said, "I am your guardian angel, Harry. I am here to let you know you are loved, you are lovable, and everything's going to be okay."

Harry's response was reassuring to some extent. I didn't know what else to do but head back to my office and process. The visual and the voice disappeared, and I went back to work.

My encounter with Harry started my journey with the angelic realm. The core message stays consistent. I am lovable. I am love. You are lovable. You are love.

This message is why I wish all of us could see ourselves as angels see us.

Over the last 25 years, I discovered something else. Some of the best of us are the hardest on ourselves. When my friend asked, "Do you know anyone who truly loves themselves?" it shocked me because I was so sure that if anyone would, she would, but like many of the most amazing healers, intuitives, and lightworkers in the world, she was her harshest critic.

Are you your harshest critic? Could you benefit from a little angel wisdom, seeing yourself as the potent font of love you are?

## YOU ARE LIGHT

Another epic lesson from my angels is knowing we are light. I'm sure you've been told to "shine your light." What does that mean to you?

My angels gave me a symbol for that concept years ago during a meditation led by a shaman. I wanted clarity on what I would do in my newly awakened state as a spiritual healer and messenger for the angels. How was I to share these new gifts? I was ready to leave my salaried job as a lawyer, but how would I support myself and my kids through college in this new direction?

I sat in a room with 100 other lightworkers, spiritual healers, and intuitives. It was a powerful group.

In the silence, I asked, "What is my real purpose, and what am I here to do? I want clarity. Let me see what I am to do."

I knew I didn't have a clue about how to practice my spiritual work in a financially sustainable way. I only knew my angel team kept encouraging me to move in that direction.

The room was dark except for a few candles around the perimeter of the room and on the altar in front of the shaman. His students played musical instruments as he led us in the meditation. The shaman's droning voice, chanting and toning at times, led me deep into a silent place inside. I asked for the clarity I was so deeply craving.

*What am I to do?*

The visual that came to me was a bright sun.

*Okay. Nice. Beautiful even, but how does that help me gain clarity?*

Nothing shifted. The bright sun was the only visual I was given.

As I inquired further, I heard, "That sun is you. You are that bright. You are to shine your light that brightly."

I thanked my guides for the message, believing it held truth, yet still not knowing exactly how I was to use it to move forward. I just knew it held deep meaning for me.

As I worked with that image in subsequent meditations, I began to see the next steps on my journey. I also discovered beliefs blocking my way. Recognizing those beliefs as invalid, I released them and moved more freely forward.

The image of the bright sun and the messages from my guides continue to help. I may not see more than one step ahead, but I know that as I focus on the light within, I feel the inspiration and the sense of empowerment to move in the right direction.

## INTERTWINING LOVE AND LIGHT

Working with both love and light is even more powerful. When I start being hard on myself, being critical for tasks undone or goals unmet, and recognize I have taken a turn south, feeling down and disappointed, I take time to turn it around. I sit, even for just five or ten minutes, and go within. I allow my heart to remember how angels see me. I call on the inner light, even if it's a small, barely glowing ember. I breathe on it until I see a flame. I allow the love and light to wash over me. I allow it to shift my energy and lift my spirits. I remember the bright light of the sun inside. I feel its warmth, its power, its vibrancy. I let it shine through my whole body, each organ, each energy center, each cell.

I remember who I am.

I am love and light, and I am here to shine.

This is also a powerful tool when external triggers bring me down. We live in times of uncertainty, divisiveness, and fearmongering. It only takes glancing at a headline in a newsfeed or thirty seconds of "breaking news" on TV to call up fear and worry. It's easy for me to drop into anxiety for my children, grandchildren, the planet, and all of humanity. So many problems and so few solutions. How are any of us going to survive?

Catching myself in a downward spiral, I sit down and first ask, *is there something I can do?* If the answer is *no, not right now,* I know the best thing I can do is shift my energy. I lay the fear at my feet and let my inner love and light do their magic. It can take a few minutes or more. When I feel the pull of my "to-do list," I remind myself this practice is the most important thing I can do in this moment. I rest in the love and light until I feel the shift, the uplift, the movement of energy. I know it's working when my body starts wanting to move, and I can feel the flow of love and light flow from top to toe. I then envision it rippling out into the world, giving all it reaches a sense of hope and inspiration. I ask, *what is the best next task for me to accomplish?* I often feel inspired to write an email I was delaying or make a phone call I put off until I felt better. Those big problems may still be unsolved, but by doing my inner work and shifting my energy, I can at least move in the direction of my soul's calling.

Can you see how powerful a simple change in perspective can be, from being too focused on your imperfections or whatever may hold you back to seeing yourself as angels see you—the love and light you are at your core?

# SEE YOURSELF AS ANGELS SEE YOU | 159

Are you ready to give yourself this gift? Are you willing to explore the possibilities of seeing yourself as angels see you? Can you imagine what would shift in your life if you could see yourself with unconditional love and know yourself as light shining as bright as the sun? Could that possibly help you overcome your challenges and move you in the direction of your dreams?

Follow the steps in the tool below and find support when you need a reminder, refill, or a sense of renewal and recharge. You are love and light. Let your love uplift the world, and your light shine brightly.

## THE TOOL

I invite you to use this tool whenever you feel less than the love and light you know you are, when you feel challenged or stuck, and especially when you feel discouraged, dismayed, or anxious about the state of the world.

You can follow along with the instructions below or listen to it in a recorded meditation at https://www.liliashoshannarae.com/resources.

Allow at least ten minutes. More, if possible, but even ten minutes can help you shift whatever is keeping you from shining your light brightly.

Notice your breath in its gentle, normal rhythm. Take three deep breaths to help you become more centered, grounded, and present in your body.

Set the intention to align your body, heart, and mind. See the energy of all three connected in a straight line through the energy centers in the core of your body.

Envision the line extending upward with a connection to what you may call Spirit, Source, Universe, or the Divine.

Follow that line down into the Earth and feel the grounding energy of our dear planet.

Bring your awareness back up to your heart space and allow it to rest there, feeling gratitude for the moment and your choice to shift whatever is challenging you.

If you have an angel you work with, ask for it to be present. If not, use your imagination to visualize an angel being present to help you for your highest good.

Ask to see yourself as the angel sees you. Imagine the angel seeing the love that is your essence. Feel the love the angel has for you, the respect, the appreciation for your being willing to be here on planet Earth in a human body to do your soul's purpose work.

Bring your awareness back into your body and feel the love coming from the angel.

Allow yourself to bask in it as if you were basking on a beach in the sunshine. Feel it bathe your whole body in that love.

Let the reminder of sunshine take you within to your own light. What do you see? Is it perhaps a small ember? Breathe on it and allow it to grow into a flame.

With each breath, allow the flame to grow. Play with the imagery. Maybe let it grow into a huge ball of light.

The ball is your light. Own it. Let it warm your whole being. Allow it to dispel and disperse anything that feels heavy or burdensome. Allow it to raise your vibration and have your whole being feel lighter and lighter.

In this moment, ask if there's anything more you are to see.

Invite the light to illuminate whatever you can let go of or move toward. Is there a next step for you to take? What if it was as brilliant as the light illuminating it?

Allow your imagination freedom to play. What is your next adventure or your next big leap?

When you feel complete, thank the angel for being with you, even if it's an angel of your imagination.

Thank yourself for being willing to take the time to shift your energy.

You may want to spend a moment or two capturing in writing any inspirations, visuals, or symbols that came to you through this exercise.

And if you want additional support, check out the resources at https://www.liliashoshannarae.com/resources

**Lilia Shoshanna Rae,** mid-career as a lawyer, experienced an angel intervention that transformed her life. Now as an author, healer, and spiritual guide, she'll help you tap into angel wisdom to live a purpose-filled life. Author of the best-selling book, The Art of Listening to Angels, Lilia is working on her second book, Living Your Brilliance, sharing angel guidance on shining your unique light and creating more love, joy, and peace in your life and the world. She has contributed to three other best-selling collaborative spiritual and transformational books.

Lilia works with healers, intuitives, and change makers. She'll help you clear blocks hindering you from sharing your gifts fully. She combines her experience as a Reiki master/teacher for over 20 years with access to the loving energy of the angelic realm in collaborative sessions that empower and inspire you.

As part of the balancing act of her life, Lilia's greatest joy comes from hanging out with her six grandchildren, newborn to eight years old, her three children and their spouses, and seeing them all light up with her dad at age 105. Her other passion in life is practicing the principles of circular leadership as part of the nonprofit, A Community of Transformation, whose vision is to be "an inspirational, heart-centered community nurturing profound transformation."

Connect with Lilia on the following sites:

Website: https://www.liliashoshannarae.com

Blog: https://www.liliashoshannarae.com/blog

Facebook: https://www.facebook.com/LiliaShoshannaRae

# TAKE AN IMPORTANT NEXT STEP

## SURROUND YOURSELF WITH OTHER ON PURPOSE WOMEN

### Ginny Robertson

*Surround yourself with women who would mention your name in a roomful of opportunities.*

~ Unknown

Does this book inspire you to act? Do you want support in moving forward?

Then you must surround yourself with other On Purpose Women.

For ideas on connecting with more On Purpose Women, keep reading, grab a pen, and get to work!

## WHAT IS AN ON PURPOSE WOMAN?

Check out my list of characteristics below. Feel free to add any that are important to you. Put a check in the Me column if that characteristic is one you embody. Next, think of women you know and write one name per trait under the Others column.

| **An On Purpose Woman** | Me | Others |
|---|---|---|
| ☐ Asks for help. | ☐ | |
| ☐ Attracts like-minded women. | ☐ | |
| ☐ Connects authentically. | ☐ | |
| ☐ Continues to learn and grow. | ☐ | |
| ☐ Embodies & welcomes change. | ☐ | |
| ☐ Embraces imperfection. | ☐ | |
| ☐ Encourages other women. | ☐ | |
| ☐ Expresses gratitude. | ☐ | |
| ☐ Feels a connection to something greater. | ☐ | |
| ☐ Goes with the flow. | ☐ | |
| ☐ Has clear boundaries. | ☐ | |
| ☐ Knows what is hers to do. | ☐ | |
| ☐ Lives with passion & purpose. | ☐ | |
| ☐ Loves herself. | ☐ | |
| ☐ Makes a difference. | ☐ | |
| ☐ Nurtures others. | ☐ | |
| ☐ Practices self-care. | ☐ | |
| ☐ Seeks & speaks her truth. | ☐ | |
| ☐ Shares abundantly. | ☐ | |
| ☐ Shines her light. | ☐ | |
| ☐ Stays true to her vision. | ☐ | |
| ☐ Takes risks. | ☐ | |
| ☐ | ☐ | |

Next, check the five qualities that matter the most to you when connecting with women. This list can become a guidepost and support you in creating connections that matter.

**Complete the following lists and answer the questions for each.**

**On Purpose Women I already know well**

- ....................................................................................................
- ....................................................................................................
- ....................................................................................................
- ....................................................................................................
- ....................................................................................................

**How can I connect with them on a deeper level?**

........................................................................................................
........................................................................................................
........................................................................................................
........................................................................................................
........................................................................................................
........................................................................................................

**On Purpose Women I want to get to know**

- ....................................................................................................
- ....................................................................................................
- ....................................................................................................
- ....................................................................................................
- ....................................................................................................

**How can I make these connections?**

........................................................................................................
........................................................................................................
........................................................................................................
........................................................................................................
........................................................................................................
........................................................................................................

**On Purpose Women I don't know.
They might be celebrities or ancestors**

- ........................................................................................................
- ........................................................................................................
- ........................................................................................................
- ........................................................................................................
- ........................................................................................................

**What are the qualities I imagine them having?**

................................................................................................................
................................................................................................................
................................................................................................................
................................................................................................................
................................................................................................................
................................................................................................................

## IN CLOSING, BE SURE TO:

- Connect with the On Purpose Women who contributed to this book by contacting us directly. Reach me here: ginnyrobertsonOPW@gmail.com
- Visit an On Purpose Woman Global Community Zoom gathering or an in-person in Columbia, Maryland, Richmond, Virginia, or Tallahassee, Florida. https://www.opwgc.com
- Join the Brave Healer Book Club, where experts from many Brave Healer publications hang out to help you. Find that here:

    https://www.facebook.com/groups/143744423674578

*The circles of women around us weave invisible nets of love that carry us when we're weak and sing with us when we are strong.*

~ Sark

# IN GRATITUDE

I've been writing in a Gratitude Journal for almost 30 years. It was essential to my daily spiritual practice, and I rarely missed a day. My gratitude practice created awareness. I looked for and saw things to be grateful for, something I might have overlooked before that awareness.

Over the past ten years, writing my daily gratitude list has become less important because I've made gratitude an integral part of my life. I live and breathe gratitude. I notice myself silently saying thank you throughout my day for things I previously took for granted. Saying thank you aloud or in writing is natural.

Gratitude opens my heart, and my open heart says Thank You!

Thank you, dear reader, for choosing this book and trusting there might be something for you here. Thank you for your vision and your dreams to make a difference through your work. We need that spark that only you can provide.

Thank you, contributing authors, for saying yes to this project. Thank you for trusting Laura and me with your words. Thank you for sharing your wisdom, as only you can, and for the ripple effect it creates.

Thank you, Laura Di Franco, for saying yes to your divine calling, sharing your words, and giving us the platform to share ours.

Thank you to our launch team members. Your encouraging words, energy, and efforts support us in getting this book out to women who would not have known about it except for you.

I have met thousands of women since beginning my journey as an on-purpose woman and spiritual entrepreneur. Some of you stepped in for a moment, and some of you are still here. Some of you have passed on, and some will arrive at the perfect time. Thank you for saying yes when you could have taken another path. I'm grateful I was paying attention.

*Thank you is the best prayer that anyone could say. I say that one a lot. Thank you expresses extreme gratitude, humility, and understanding.*

~ Alice Walker

# ABOUT THE AUTHOR

I'm **Ginny Robertson,** the woman behind the On Purpose Woman Global Community and On Purpose Woman Magazine.

My inspiration for my business and the rest of my life is to "Connect Women Around the World to Their Gifts, Their Purpose & Each Other."

I support women, wherever you are in life, with opportunities for deep connection, more visibility, and becoming more comfortable with playing a more significant role on the planet - whatever that means for you.

Everything I do is about shining a light and supporting you in using your voice to be seen and heard so you can share your gifts and make your unique difference.

**There is always a seat at our table.**

## CONNECT WITH THE ON PURPOSE WOMAN GLOBAL COMMUNITY & MAGAZINE

- Join our Email list and receive our gift of "The On Purpose Woman Booklet." It's a PDF that includes tips for:
  - Networking with Heart: Creating Connections that Matter
  - Standing in the Spotlight: The Courage to be Seen & Heard
    bit.ly/3Xy9Lb5

- Become a paid member of the community and use our member features to grow your business. It's just $19/month of $195 for the year. https://opwgc.com/join/

- Attend one of our nine online gatherings or our in-person meetings in Columbia, Maryland, Richmond, Virginia, and Tallahassee, Florida. https://opwgc.com/about-our-gatherings/

- Read On Purpose Woman Magazine: https://opwgc.com/magazine/

- Join the On Purpose Woman Global Community on Facebook. https://www.facebook.com/groups/onpurposenetworkingforwomen
- Speak at an On Purpose Woman Zoom or in-person meeting. Contact ginnyrobertsonopw@gmail.com
- Submit an Article to On Purpose Woman Magazine. https://opwgc.com/submission-guidelines/
- Advertise in On Purpose Woman Magazine: https://opwgc.com/advertise-with-opw-magazine/
- Be the Cover Artist for On Purpose Woman Magazine. https://opwgc.com/submission-guidelines/
- Be interviewed on our Real Women Real Purpose Talk Show live on Facebook in our On Purpose Woman Global Community group. Check out those interviews and our meeting speakers on our YouTube channel. Support the channel by subscribing. https://www.youtube.com/c/OnPurposeWomanGlobalCommunity

I also invite you to reach out with any questions or comments about what I've written throughout this book. Let me know how I can support you in your growth as a spiritual entrepreneur.

Ginny

*Connection: The power that exists between people when they feel seen, heard, and valued.*

~ Brene Brown